women on the

# buddhist

path

women on the

# buddhist

path

Martine Batchelor

Edited by Gill Farrer-Halls

Thorsons

Thorsons
An Imprint of HarperCollins*Publishers*
77–85 Fulham Palace Road
Hammersmith, London w6 8jb

The Thorsons website address is:
www.thorsons.com

and *Thorsons*
are trademarks of
HarperCollins*Publishers* Ltd

First published as *Walking on Lotus Flowers*
in 1996 by Thorsons
This edition published by Thorsons in 2002

3 5 7 9 10 8 6 4 2

© Martine Batchelor 1996

Martine Batchelor asserts the moral right
to be identified as the author of this work

A catalogue record for this book
is available from the British Library

ISBN 0 00 713319 7

Printed in Great Britain by
Creative Print & Design, Ebbw Vale, Wales

Photo p. 104 by Phil Borges

To my mother, Lea Fages

# contents

## Part Four: Healing the World

# acknowledgements

I would like to thank deeply all the nuns and laywomen who are in this book for their availability, their wisdom and compassion. I have a debt of profound gratitude to all the nuns, monks and laypeople who kindly helped me on my travels with translation, information, food, lodging and support. I would like to mention especially the Koo family, Mr and Mrs Dodds, Paul and Suil Jaffe, Chatsumarn Kabilsingh and Sheryl Keller. I would like to thank Susan Blake for her enthusiasm in the early stages of the editing, Gill Farrer-Halls for her skills and the joy of working with her, and Liz Puttick at HarperCollins for her interest and support. To finish I would like to thank my husband, Stephen, for his love, support and help throughout the project.

This book would not have been possible without generous grants from the Korea Foundation, the Spalding Trust and the International Society for Ecology and Culture.

# introduction

'How can I meditate when I am so busy with my work and family?' 'How can I reconcile activity with stillness?' 'Are there any Buddhist nuns?' 'Can you find great female spiritual teachers in the Buddhist tradition?'

As a meditation teacher and former Buddhist nun, I have been asked these questions countless times. So I decided to compile a book drawn from the living experiences of contemporary women, showing how a meditative attitude can influence a diverse range of lifestyles and activities. Indeed, I discovered many great nuns and Buddhist women teachers today.

From conception to completion this book was a long drawn-out adventure. I had to believe I could do it and find the financial support to make it happen. I wrote to two grant-giving organizations, but not much happened, so I gave up. Then suddenly, after a long time, both grants came together within a week, plus a further grant from another organization. I was stunned; and I had to do it!

My travels took me from my doorstep, where I interviewed Western women, to the roots of Buddhism in Korea, Japan, Taiwan and Thailand. I was amazed and elated by the riches and array of lifestyles I found. Some women I knew already and had corresponded with, but I encountered so many more it became difficult to choose who would be in the book. I had 40 interviews, all with quite extraordinary women, but realized I had to confine myself to 18, for reasons of space, and the quality of each interview became the decisive factor. However, in a certain way they all speak for each other.

When I interviewed people I felt like a beginner, asking simple, relevant and practical questions. Some interviews were in English; the easiest to deal with. Many were in Korean; I hope my translation conveys the person behind the words. Others were translated by someone else at the time from Japanese, Chinese and Thai. Every chapter tells a story and gives advice on meditation in the personal voice and through the distinctive experience of each woman.

Meeting these Buddhist women was a learning process which kept developing as I worked on the interviews, translating, transcribing, typing and editing. I never became bored because there was so much freshness and wisdom; such good stories. I still wonder if I would have the courage and faith of Ani Tenzin Palmo when faced by a blizzard in the Himalayas, or Ayya Khema's calm acceptance when confronted with cancer.

I remain inspired by Haeju Sunim, who tells us we are all Buddhas and the only way to live is to display the compassion and wisdom of a Buddha; no need to wait for another time, another retreat, another life. I am still enthused by I Tsao Fashih, who tried convincing me to pray to be reborn in the Pure Land. She could see I was not very keen, but was so joyful, generous and funny that I left her feeling perhaps I might be walking on lotus flowers, and wouldn't life be amazing experienced that way!

I chuckle again at the insouciance with which Maechee Pathomwan regarded a snake appearing on her lap, compared to the fear a ghost would have caused her. I marvel at the surrealist imagination of Yahne Le Toumelin. I am touched by the simplicity of Zen painter Okbong Sunim and the compassion of Jonmok Sunim, a nun disc jockey and social worker.

Some of their experiences are similar to mine. Like Sister Chan Khong, I was told to pray to be reborn as a man; like her I discard it as nonsense and do not think it relevant advice, however kindly meant by however saintly and enlightened a person. But we must not forget the Buddha was revolutionary when he said everybody was equal in awakening. This book proves his point by showing women taking hold of their spiritual path and displaying a wide spectrum of meditative achievements.

Many books have been written about women and Buddhism from a feminist, sociological, religious, cultural or historical point of view. I wanted to approach this subject from a different angle, that of meditative experience and everyday life. Some of the women in this book are at the forefront of the debate in the West. But I wanted to know more about their actual lives than their ideas; how did they live day to day as Buddhists? What did it mean for them at an experiential level to be a Buddhist woman practitioner?

In the East whenever I broached the subject of women and Buddhism or nuns versus monks, the women felt they were equal. Myongsong Sunim, for example, says that monks and nuns are the two wings of a bird – the bird needs both wings in order to fly. And indeed, in their experience they have been equal, achieving the same as any man or monk in their practice and status. Even when conditions seemed to be against them, like in Thailand, this did not stop Maechee Pathomwan from becoming a nun, practising and becoming a respected teacher.

I need to say something about the status of nuns in Buddhism. This varies according to the social and historical conditions in each country and makes too long a story to relate here. So I have abbreviated it thus: Korean nuns are 90 per cent equal to monks, Japanese nuns 60 per cent, Taiwanese nuns 85 per cent, Thai nuns 15 per cent, Tibetan nuns 45 per cent. For example, Korean nuns take the full ordination with 338 precepts, whilst Thai nuns barely have an ordination at all, with only eight or 10 precepts.

Unsurprisingly, the Korean nuns are better supported and have more opportunities for training and studying. But what impressed and reassured me was that no matter how difficult and poor the conditions, the women practitioners I met were able to transcend them, lead full lives and become teachers in their own right, like Maechee Pathomwan in Thailand and Pang Kwihi, a paraplegic novelist in Korea.

I tried to include many Buddhist traditions to show the wide range of meditative techniques, and I found a multiplicity of approaches and possibilities. The Buddhist path is diverse; there is a little of everything for everybody. However, the common thread running through this book is *mindfulness*, a creative awareness which if applied and cultivated helps us to see clearly, transforming the way we are and how we live.

These women's lives tell us to believe in ourselves and our potential, whether we are a woman or a man, have a high or low status, are healthy or handicapped. The message is we can but give it a good try. These women made me laugh, cry and ponder; made me wiser and more open to the inexhaustible possibilities life offers on the spiritual path. I hope they touch your lives in the same way.

# 1

# The Meditative Path

# 1

## the space between thoughts
### Ani Tenzin Palmo

Ani Tenzin Palmo was born in 1943 in England. She went to India in 1964 and spent a total of 24 years there. She spent six years in Dalhousie in the monastery of her lama (teacher) and 18 in Lahul (near Ladakh, northern India, Himalayan region), including 12 years in solitary retreat in a cave, before returning to Europe to live in Assisi, Italy, in 1988. Although a hermit by temperament, Ani Palmo is wonderfully friendly, direct and a great joy to talk with.

## Start from Where You Are

You must obviously start from where you are. Nobody in the world can just sit down and immediately meditate. Westerners have the idea that Asians just sit down and then everything appears at once in its intrinsic perfection. This is not true, and I have asked many yogis and lamas about this. They all spoke of how difficult it was in the beginning and how they really had to apply themselves. So do not be discouraged.

If you are in deep pain mentally you might find it quite difficult to meditate at the beginning. There might be alternative ways to proceed, by other methods or through introspection. One thing is very important: do not think that practice is something you do only when you are sitting on your cushion.

## Practice Moment to Moment

Westerners are often frustrated because of feeling they have no time for practice. They are always saying: 'We have to work, we do not have any time to sit.' They have the idea it is only practice when they are sitting saying mantras or doing some kind of breathing meditation. This is not the case. Practice is something you do moment to moment, all through the day. It is the way you relate to the people you meet. It is the way you drink your tea, approach your work and how you become more aware of your internal responses to things. It is a matter of waking up. Mostly we live our lives in a kind of sleepwalking state.

The practice is [*snapping her fingers*] to wake up and develop clarity and alertness and at the same time love, kindness and consideration. You are kind not just to all sentient beings in the 10 directions as a wish, but practically to the person who is next to you, your wife or husband, your children, colleagues at work, the stranger you meet on the bus, to anybody. You are just aware that these people are suffering as you are suffering.

That extra smile, that extra kindness can mean so much to people. This is practice.

It is not how many millions of mantras you say. This is so irrelevant. I feel it is a big mistake when people get the idea that unless they go into long retreats and do millions of different kinds of practices they are not going to get anywhere. True practice on the Bodhisattva path has very little to do with that but an enormous amount to do with the quality of our every-day lives and our relationships.

In everyday life my practice is to see each person I meet as dear to themselves and therefore that person is important. It does not matter who they are, how old or how young. Each person is terribly important to themselves. We should respect that. I also try to give people space to be as they are without immediately judging or evaluating them.

Each person is unique and wonderful in their own way. It is like a dance where everyone dances their own dance. It is also like a symphony in which every person is playing their own instrument, their own variation on a theme. People do not have to act in a certain prescribed way; they are free to be themselves in whatever way they are. If you can appreciate that, you can feel joy in whatever they are doing.

I like to have periods of solitude, but this is not because I do not like people. In solitude I feel a greater sense of identity with the world. I do not forget the world at all. On the contrary, I find these periods of isolation are beneficial in helping me to be open in my relationships with other people and considerate of the fact that there are other people.

## 'You Are a Kagyupa'

I started practising in London in 1961 when I became a Buddhist at the age of 18. After six months I joined the Buddhist Society. They had a basic Buddhist class and a meditation class.

I started off as a Theravada and studied at the Sinhalese Vihara. In those days, people were either Theravada or Zen. Tibetan Buddhism was regarded as very degenerate and debased, with black magic and weird sexual practices – practically not Buddhism at all and absolutely nothing I would want to have anything to do with. But one day I read a book and at the end there was a small section on Tibetan Buddhism. It said: 'In Tibet there were four sects: Nyingmapa, Sakyapa, Kagyupa and Gelugpa.'

As I read that, something inside me said: 'You are a Kagyupa.' I wondered what to do with this discovery and asked someone who knew about Tibetan Buddhism, 'What about this "Kagyupa"?' She suggested I read Milarepa and she handed me Evans-Wentz's translation of the life of Mila. It completely changed my whole perception and I realized I had to find a teacher, which meant going to India.

Meantime Chögyam Trungpa Rinpoche had turned up with Akong Rinpoche from India and he gave me some meditation instructions. One day, he said to me: 'You might find this hard to believe, but in Tibet I was quite a high lama. I never thought it would come to this, but please can I teach you meditation? I must have one disciple.'

I replied it was fine by me and he started teaching me meditation. It was like Mahamudra, sitting down, letting the mind relax, standing back and looking at the coming and going of thoughts.

## Mahamudra

Mahamudra is extremely simple and this is probably its difficulty. It basically entails sitting with the mind relaxed and simultaneously maintaining a keen alertness and awareness. You just practise being aware of the coming and going of your thoughts, not trying to produce or impede them, or becoming

interested in them. You just stay with them, looki
through them. Thoughts by nature are quite transpare
this begins to develop, thoughts begin to slow down
the mind is relaxed. When thoughts become slower, in t
between two thoughts, when your awareness is very clear, you
see that which lies between and behind the thoughts. This
intense clarity is spaciousness and awareness, the true nature of
mind.

You can do Mahamudra as your sole practice. Then it is
useful to have an experienced teacher nearby, because it is
very easy to meander along and you need someone to question you: 'What has happened? How is this? Was it like this,
was it like that?' This keeps the practice sharp and directed.
Otherwise Mahamudra is done at the end of the main visualization practice. Then you allow the mind just to relax into its
innate emptiness and have awareness of that. This spaciousness, clarity and awareness you see between thoughts, this is
the emptiness of mind.

If your awareness is very keen at this point, you see it. To say
you 'see' it could be misleading, though, because at this point
there is no seeing. This is what Mahamudra is all about.

Of course, having realized that state, you begin to analyse it
in true Buddhist fashion: the awareness, the thought and the
stillness behind the thought, are they the same, are they different? If they are different, in what way are they different? If they
are the same, in what way are they the same? You begin to
question in order to understand the experience. In Buddhist
practice this is very important; you not only have the experience, but also understand it by questioning.


## The Dharma Is So Precious

I always wanted to be a nun. As a child I was drawn to the idea
of contemplative orders like the Carmelites, the sort of place

you enter, doors clang behind you and you never come out. Unfortunately I did not believe in the idea of a personal God and Christianity left me cold. When I first heard about Buddhism, people mentioned only monks and I felt sad there were no nuns. When I finally saw nuns mentioned somewhere I was immediately overjoyed and knew it was what I wanted to be.

Outwardly I did not look like a nun at all. I was always running around wearing pretty clothes and having lots of boyfriends – not the type who was going to end up as a nun. When I met my lama, however, it was obvious that the only thing I wanted was to be with him and completely devote my life to the dharma [the Buddha's teaching]. I asked him if I could become a nun and he ordained me about three weeks after I met him.

The dharma felt so infinitely precious I could not waste any time and for me anything else but practising the dharma was a waste of time. I did not want to be distracted by other considerations; I just wanted to spend my life with my lama, practising the dharma to the best of my abilities. I would resent my emotions being involved with an ordinary man. If I wanted to really love someone, then I wanted to love my lama and that was more than enough. Of course when I was with him, I worked. I was his secretary and also taught English to the young monks. I worked 12 hours a day. Because it was for my lama, it was also the dharma.

My relationships with men changed completely. Being a nun has allowed me to have close relationships with men without any sexual connotations. They feel free around me. When I meet men, I think of them as my friends or my brothers, so there simply is no problem. This makes our relationships spacious and open and I am grateful for that.

In all the years I have been a nun I have never for one second regretted it. I have an enormous respect and love for the ordained sangha [community]. The feeling that this is a tradition which goes all the way back to the Buddha himself gives me an incredible sense of strength and joy. The nuns and monks are meant to be an example of the dharma life well lived.

The West needs a small sangha of really dedicated people, monks and nuns, to be the focal point of a well-lived dharma life. The whole point of being a monk or nun is that with one sweep it clears away so many of the concerns which preoccupy most people's lives: relationships with the opposite sex, falling in love, feeling jealous, insecure, getting married, having children. These are very important things, but nonetheless they can detract from the energy and emotional power which could be given to dharma practice.

Not everyone should become a nun or monk and it is absolutely ridiculous to think you can only practise the dharma if you are a monk or nun. But there is no doubt the Buddha started the sangha because it creates a way of life which enables people to have the freedom, space and time to dedicate themselves to as much dharma practice as they wish.

## A Hermit's Life

My lama said to me: 'For you, it is better to be alone.' Whenever I suggested living with anybody else, with another nun, he always said: 'No, for you, it is better to stay alone.'

When I first went to Lahul, I lived within a monastery complex although I lived alone in a house, as did everybody else in that monastery. There were both monks and nuns. On one level we got along very well and there were no problems. However, it was not ideal for doing retreat because I was usually the only one in retreat and my house was in the middle of the monastery complex. Everybody followed their usual activities, having parties and long conversations on the roof-tops from house to house, so it was not very peaceful.

I decided I needed to be more isolated. Eventually I heard about a cave and went to stay there. It was an ideal situation and I had nobody else to blame except myself if things did not go well. There is no doubt that for intense practice either you should be completely alone or together with other people also doing that practice. In other circumstances it becomes much more difficult.

I was frequently snowed in for a long time each year, but I never felt lonely. On the contrary, I was often filled with the thought that there was nowhere else on Earth I would rather be and nothing else in the world I would rather be doing. There was an enormous sense of fitness and rightness about what I was doing.

The only time in my life I ever did feel lonely was when I was living with my lama in his monastery of 80 monks and I was the only nun and only foreigner. Everybody was living together as a community and I was always on the outside. When I actually lived alone I never felt lonely for a moment. It was a great joy to feel I had all this time and space in which to concentrate completely on my practice without external distractions. If I occasionally felt slightly bored, I would read an inspiring dharma book.

I love being alone. I like being with other people, but not for an extended length of time, whereas I could be alone for ever and ever and it would never bore me. I think perhaps it is because when I am with other people I tend to compromise, to fit in with whatever is happening and thus not to be completely true to myself. When I am by myself I can arrange my own day and be true to myself and the practice. It also gives me a great sense of spaciousness.

Many people have difficulties when they go into solitary retreat, but I think it is a matter of which type of mind you have. Some people who stayed in my cave when I was not there had a lot of problems. In the end they spent most of their time in the monastery and even down in the village. They could not stay in the cave by themselves. They 'spaced out' too much, or got caught in fantasies or a lot of fears which they did not know how to deal with.

Some people think that living alone and practising is escapism, but in fact it is the one time you can really face reality because there is nowhere to escape to. Whatever comes up, you cannot turn on the television, talk to your neighbour, run away or do anything, you just have to sit there and face it. Whether it is some internal problem or external problem, there is only you to deal with it. Personally, I found that very strengthening, because I discovered that in fact I am far more resourceful than I had previously realized.

### 'Tunnel Out!'

One year there was a freak blizzard which blew for seven days and seven nights. It caused vast avalanches all over Lahul, many villages were completely destroyed, thousand of trees were uprooted and hundreds of people died. I was trapped in the cave under tons of snow. The chimney to my stove broke so I could not light a fire. Everything was totally black inside and when I opened the door there was just this wall of ice.

I was trapped in this very small space. I thought the air was getting less and less and truly felt I was going to die. I had time to think about it. Looking back, it was interesting because I did not panic, nor get claustrophobic; I was very calm, perfectly accepting. I realized that the only thing that really mattered when it came to the crunch was the lama; he was the one refuge.

I prayed to him from the depth of my heart to take care of me in the bardo [intermediate state between death and rebirth] and as I did that, I heard a voice inside me saying, 'Tunnel out!' So I started to dig out the snow from the door. Of course I had to bring the snow into the cave, there was nowhere else. At first I used a shovel, then after a while, as I began to make a tunnel, I used a saucepan lid and after this my hand. It took about an hour or so. For a time I was in this terribly tiny constricted little ice tube. It was black down below and it was black in front.

Eventually the tunnel began to get light and I came out. There was so much snow you could not see the cave at all. I could not see any trees, nor the top of my 10-foot (3m) pole, just this completely white space, still blizzardy.

I had to clear the snow out of the cave, so I crawled back into the tunnel. When I went back in my eyes were very painful and bright red, as if someone had thrown hot sands into them. They were streaming and I realized I had become snow-blind. Anyway, I survived.

The next day the snow had built up again and I had to dig it out again. I did this three times and eventually the blizzard finished. Eventually, about a month later, a monk came over from the monastery and told me the villages had been destroyed. Probably I was the safest person, living in this cave which could not be destroyed. I realized that in this time of great challenge I had had only my own inner and outer resources. There was nobody I could have shared it with, I had to go through it by myself and I did it perfectly competently.

## The Inner TV Channel

I did retreats usually from November to May or June. May usually, because by that time the snow was beginning to melt and I had to pay more attention to that, so it was not really possible to continue a strict retreat anymore. What I did between May and November varied. I had the garden to attend to, also getting in supplies, arranging for wood, collecting it, applying mud to insulate the cave and so on. Sometimes people would come. It was also a time when I would read more, do more painting.

Then in October I would go to Tashijong to visit my lama and on the way back I would sometimes stay in Manali to get supplies. As a matter of course I always do early morning and evening practices when I am busy during the day.

Once I did a three-year retreat but it was interrupted at the end, so it was actually two years and nine months. During that retreat, a Lahuli brought supplies to me once a year.

Internally, the main problem was a certain boredom with the practice at times. Throughout the 12 years I lived in the cave, this always happened. At the beginning of the retreat, after about two weeks, there would be a feeling of: 'Oh no! I have to keep doing this for so many months!' After all, it is like watching the same television programme, four times a day, week after week, month after month. At a certain point I would feel, 'Oh no, not again!'

Because there was no one there to encourage me or to talk about it with to break the monotony, again I would have to deal with it by myself. I found the only way was just not to give in and to keep going. After a while I recognized the boredom, so it was not a problem anymore. I just kept going and kept to the routine. It was essential not to break it, not to ask myself whether I felt like doing it. After a while, invariably the practice took up its own momentum again. Then it was on a higher plateau and became extremely interesting, almost compelling. By the end of the retreat I invariably felt more enthusiastic about the practice than when I started.

In the end the problem became more the idea than the actuality: the thought of how I was going to be able to bear to do it, while still knowing that in fact I did enjoy it.

## A Refuge and a Joy

With meditation, people tend to be too ambitious at the beginning and feel they should sit every day for an hour. What usually happens is that they cannot sustain their concentration for an hour, so become bored and discouraged. After a while, despite their best intentions, they give up. I think it is better to start by doing 10 or 20 minutes a day.

Begin by having a devotional picture of whatever it is that inspires you and offer incense or a candle to put yourself in the right frame of mind. Sit down and feel that for this short time you are going to completely devote yourself to this practice, which is not just for yourself but will benefit everybody you come into contact with. This is only a short time, but it is a very special time, reserved just for your practice.

Whatever thoughts, cares or worries come up, just let them go. Do something simple like sitting and watching the breath. The Buddha attained enlightenment watching his breath. It is not a baby's practice, it is for everybody, and can lead onwards and onwards. There is no end to it.

So sit quietly, watching the incoming and outgoing of the breath, perhaps at the nostrils or the abdomen, wherever it feels comfortable. Just try to be with the breath, with the flow, and do not worry if the mind goes away. It does not matter. We should not expect to be perfect right away; that is pride. Stay with the flow of the breath. If the mind goes away, just quietly bring it back. If it goes away again, bring it back again and again. Bringing the mind back again is the practice.

Practise like this for 10 or 20 minutes. Even if your concentration is going well and becoming strong, let it finish. Try to finish on an up note rather than keeping going until you get restless. If you do, next time there will be a slight disinclination to sit again. If you stop while you would really like it to go on longer, then there will be a feeling of enthusiasm and pleasure in sitting again. Meditation should not be an ordeal, it should be a refuge and a joy.

## A Process of Discovery

My meditation of course has deepened and become much clearer over the years. People talk about what you gain from meditation, but it seems to me it is not a matter of what you gain but of what you lose. Meditation is a process of uncovering and discovering what you have always really known. You do not discover something new; you merely realize what you have already known, but without ever having understood that you knew it. We know everything, but just do not realize it. Realizing what we have always been, what we already know, is to my mind what it is all about. Meditation opens the access to our own inner knowledge and clears away the obscurations so we can see clearly.

Everybody as they carry on practising has their own unique difficulty. However, any meditation that is carried out in a manner which is relaxed and at the same time alert will not deviate. The problem is that often it is easy to get into a meditation which seems to be flowing well. There is great peacefulness, but the mind is in fact quite dull. You can meditate like this for hours quite blissfully, but actually it is a kind of somnolence.

A real indication that the meditation is correct is when the mind is very bright, very clear and intensely awake, and at the same time extremely relaxed and soft. It is important to keep the balance. If you have that balance, you know it. In this poised state, alert and bright, you cannot go wrong.

## A Teacher Points the Way

I do not think it is essential to have a teacher. If you are in a situation where there is none, this cannot be an excuse not to start practising. There are plenty of books and with a bit of common sense you can certainly go quite a long way without a teacher.

However, there is no doubt that having a true teacher facilitates everything enormously. If you are going on a journey, you can travel by yourself, but having a guide who has been there before and knows the terrain well obviously makes the journey quicker and easier. You are assured of not taking any false roads and have no worries because you know you are secure. This is what a teacher is for, to point out the way for you. They do not do it for you, nobody does it for you. All they can do is to advise in which direction you should walk.

With my own teacher, it was wonderful. I knew from the beginning, on just hearing his name, that he was my teacher. He never doubted for one moment that I was his disciple, so from the beginning it was a very close relationship. He was a wonderful lama and I am deeply grateful to him, beyond words, that he was.

He taught me more in the sense of being there than giving teaching. He usually would indicate what practices I should be doing and give me the empowerment for them. Then I would go and get the actual teachings from yogis living in the monastery. The lama is there for his presence, direction and blessings. I learned an enormous amount from Rinpoche just from being with him. The presence of a true master is beyond words, an incredible thing – the living embodiment of what we are striving for. You know it is possible because he is there showing you how it should be, how it is.

Whatever I wanted to do in my practice, I could ask Rinpoche what he thought and he would say either that it was not necessary or that it was good. This gave me a tremendous impetus. If the lama said: 'This is very good, do it,' I could go straight ahead and put all my energy into it without any worries.

In difficult times, for example when I was living alone doing my practices, the lama was always there to be prayed to. If I had any problems, I only had to concentrate and pray to

Rinpoche for the answer to come. Certainly for me it was indispensable to have my teacher. The lama is always in my heart.

Nowadays inspiration really comes from the practice itself. At this point, even if I wanted to give it all up, I could not, it is so much a part of myself. The more I practise, the more I appreciate how incredibly unique and wonderful the dharma is. I am so intensely grateful to the Buddha for having taught it.

# 2
## a zen journey
# Songgyong Sunim

I was fortunate to spend 10 years as a Zen Buddhist nun in Korea and one of my fondest recollections was of meeting Songgyong Sunim, the leader of the meditation hall in Naewon Sa, one of the principal Zen nunneries. She was tiny and stooped but remarkably energetic for her 80 years. When she was not leading the meditation in the Zen hall, she was busy gathering acorns or performing other chores for the community.

# A Hard Life

I was born on 2 May 1903 in a little village near the city of Ch'ongju. We were poor, farming peasants, and when I was nine my mother died. I had an older brother and sister and a younger sister of five. Our father grieved terribly over our mother's death but failed to take good care of us. Life became very difficult and finally it was so bad I decided to kill myself. But as soon as I made that decision, I heard a voice from the sky say: 'Your affinity with the Buddha is great. Why end your life?' I understood this to mean I should become a nun.

So at 18 I made my way to a nunnery called Yongun Am near the monastery of Magok Sa. At first I was refused admission because I was so small. Then an elderly nun, Inu Sunim, said that although I was small, otherwise I looked all right. Thus I was accepted.

The following year the nuns shaved my head and I received ordination. My preceptress was called Myongdok Sunim. She travelled a great deal from nunnery to nunnery in order to further her meditation practice. Her own preceptress happened to be Inu Sunim, who thus became my elder. She agreed to take charge of me and for many years I served as her attendant.

My life was hard. I had to wash clothes, prepare food, chop wood and make fires. Sometimes I even had to go and cut wood in the forest and carry it on a frame on my back. I was very dismayed at having to do this kind of work, because in the villages this was normally the work of men. Once I remember thinking life in the nunnery was even worse than life in the village and I threw down the carrying-frame in disgust. Then I sat down and cried. Since I had damaged the frame slightly, my elder asked me what had happened. I told her: 'I am done with that kind of work! I am too small! I am a nun. Why should I do it?' After that she never asked me to do such things again.

## The Need to Meditate

I stayed at Yongun Am until I was 33. At that time the Japanese were occupying the whole country and were causing many difficulties for the Buddhist community. As a result the Buddhist Order suggested that in order to consolidate the teachings, the great Zen monks of the time should become abbots of the main temples. As part of this policy, Master Mangong, the Zen Master of Chonghye Sa near Sudok Sa, was appointed abbot of Magok Sa for three years.

On his first visit he encouraged the monks to build a Zen hall. He said abruptly: 'Since you are monks, how is it you idle away your lives without practising meditation?'

I was 32 when I heard this and had never heard anything like it before. It was extraordinary and inspired me with great determination to practise. Afterwards I pondered quietly and realized the role of monks and nuns was very different from what I had been led to believe.

Master Mangong's talks would always accord with his audience. To practitioners, he would talk about meditation; to students of the sutras he would talk about the *Heart Sutra*, urging them both to understand its literal meaning as well as to awaken to its deeper meaning through practice.

I realized I wanted to find a nunnery near his usual place of residence, Chonghye Sa, 100 kilometres [62 miles] northwest of Magok Sa. On learning of my wishes, my elder refused to let me go. I explained that I wanted to learn more about the true role of a nun. But she countered by saying that to go would not be in accordance with that role. She also questioned my ability to understand dharma talks, since I had never heard any before. She added that one should just live as one lives – there was nothing more to it than that. She even tried to prevent me from leaving by offering me a special position in the nunnery, but it was to no avail. Nothing could deter me now and I begged her for four days. Finally she gave in and told me I could go for a visit. Without giving me money or quilts, she helped me pack, telling me to have a look and come back soon.

## Communal Life

The monastery of Chonghye Sa was like another world. When I saw the meditation hall, I felt that the Buddha himself lived there. I wanted to stay at a nearby nun's Zen hall, Kyongsong Am, but had no money for my food. In those days [1936], a nun or monk had to provide one *mal* [18 kilos/40lb] of rice per month, amounting to three *mal* per meditation season. In Kyongsong Am this system of payment stopped shortly after I arrived.

Although I had neither rice nor money, they offered me the job of preparing the side dishes in the kitchen for a year. I accepted this and in return I was permitted to practise in the Zen hall with the other nuns. During that time, I heard dharma talks by Mangong Sunim and also by Pophui Sunim, an elderly nun who was the senior advisor at Kyongsong Am.

At the end of the year my elder appeared in Kyongsong Am, insisting she could not live without me, that I alone was capable of serving her properly. She said if I did not return with her, she would come and live with me at Kyongsong Am. I refused to return to that kind of existence since Mangong Sunim clearly did not approve of this way of life for monks and nuns. He used to say living like that would send us to hell after death. So I entreated her to spend a meditation season there with me, and she did.

Strangely enough, the communal life of the Zen hall appealed to her. She commented on how very practical and eco-nomical it was to live together in this way. And since she medi-tated in the Zen hall and ate formally with the assembly, it was no longer necessary for me to be her attendant. All I had to do was help her wash her clothes and do some small chores. Sitting in meditation was new to her but she developed real faith and 'great determination' to practise arose within her.

The following year, at the end of the summer period of meditation, my preceptress showed up. At that time she was living in the Zen hall of Yunp'il Am, a nunnery near Mungyong, in the northeastern part of South Korea. She asked me if I wanted to join her there. I accepted, overjoyed at the prospect of spending more time with her.

## A Shocking Visit

Before leaving, however, I decided I should learn more about the *hwadu* [literally 'head of speech', the crucial part of a koan] from Master Mangong. I had never really had the opportunity to ask him questions, because I had always been so busy in the kitchen. Although I had listened to his dharma lectures and had tried to put into practice what he advised, I had usually given up after a short while. As yet I had not seriously taken up a *hwadu*. Master Mangong usually taught the *hwadus* 'The thousand things return to the one. Where does the one return?', 'No!' or 'What is it?' I realized that if I really wanted to meditate I had to have my own *hwadu*.

So one day I visited Master Mangong in his room. He was sitting there alone. I bowed three times and told him: 'I would like to have a *hwadu*. Please teach me a *hwadu*.'

Although he had seen me enter, he had still not looked up. He just sat there with his eyes closed. I felt very nervous and wondered if he was behaving in this way because he thought that I, being so small, could not practise. I became sad and began to think of all my shortcomings.

Then, after about 30 minutes of silence, I decided to leave. At that moment he suddenly opened his eyes wide and shouted:

'Since you are incapable of knowing where is the head or the tail, what kind of "head of speech" are you talking about?'

I was so surprised by this outburst that my chest felt heavy and my heart pounded as if I had been struck by a ball. I did not know what to do. I felt so distressed to have been given a scolding instead of a *hwadu* that I scurried out of the back door without asking him anything more.

Shortly afterwards I left with my preceptress. I was very glad to go with her, but it felt like there was a coagulated mass in my chest brought about by the shock of my encounter with Master Mangong. I was still overwhelmed by distress and concern about not having a *hwadu*.

Not long after we arrived at Yunp'il Am, Ch'ongam Sunim, a disciple of Master Mangong, visited the nunnery from Taesong Am, the main monastery nearby, where he held the post of Zen advisor. I asked him if he would teach me a little about a *hwadu* so I could practise meditation properly. He exclaimed: 'If you did not learn a *hwadu* from Master Mangong, from whom will you ever learn?'

This distressed me even more and I pondered on the fact that for a second time a great monk was rebuking me. Once more I was overwhelmed with anxiety and shame.


## Vivid Clarity

A few days later the meditation season began. Thirty nuns had gathered in the Zen hall, all diligent meditators. We decided to begin with a 30-day period of strenuous meditation. But I could not think of practising seriously any more, I just felt great distress and shame, thinking everyone was probably wondering what on Earth I was doing during the meditation periods. I had to make tea in the mornings, but for the rest of the time I sat in meditation. Sometimes I experienced distressing thoughts, sometimes doubts like 'Why can't I practise like the others?'

and 'Why do the monks always rebuke me and not give me a *hwadu?*'

For the next 21 days this mind of self-reproach did not abate. I lost the need to sleep and spoke to no one. Then I found myself in a state of vivid clarity. At 11.30 the other nuns would go to sleep in the meditation hall in their respective places, but I would go to the side room and meditate all night. Slowly, a vivid and tranquil state of mind arose. All distracted thoughts dissolved and only clarity and quiescence remained. Occasionally the question 'What is it?' would arise. All trace of distress disappeared, leaving the mind clear and pure.

Suddenly a single thought pierced right through me, all the way up to the top of my head. The thought was so powerful that a voice came out of me which said: 'Since originally there is no head or tail, where could either of them be?'

## No Hindrances

Shortly after this, Ch'ongam Sunim came to Yunp'il Am. I told him the self-reproach had pierced through me to the point where I felt I could toss the great masters over my shoulder. He explained that this was the great doubt on the point of bursting. It still had to grow more before it burst, but once it had then the practice would progress easily.

The following day he pinned up a notice on the wall of the Zen hall which read: 'Riding the bottomless iron boat, there is no hindrance to crossing the land.'

When I read this, it suddenly occurred to me that in the midst of mind there are no hindrances. Only the doubt remained and even that would disappear! The next time we met I told him how I understood the bottomless iron boat to be the mind. I added that because, fundamentally, the mind has no hindrances, it has no difficulties in crossing the land.

He replied that the doubt had now burst and my practice

was going well. It seemed this was the first time he had come across a nun whose doubt had burst so greatly and it prompted him to return to Chonghye Sa to practise with even greater vigour under Master Mangong. Apparently he was afraid of being surpassed in his practice by a nun.

I now had no distracted thoughts at all; my mind was absolutely clear and quiet and great faith was arising. I was pleased with the faith which poured out of me and could think of nothing except practising meditation.

During that summer's meditation season, an event from one of my past lives suddenly appeared. I saw that in a past life I had been an intelligent and handsome monk. I also saw a very pretty girl who had been born from the heavenly realm and become a nun. I caused this nun to break her precepts. I then died at the age of 50 and was reborn small and ugly but with a pure mind. After the beautiful nun died, she was reborn as the nun who became my elder.

While I was with my elder I had often wondered why, regardless of my behaviour, she had sometimes liked me and sometimes not. After this vision I understood it was because I had made her break her precepts in a previous life. I did not know whether to take this vision seriously or not, yet felt thoroughly happy about it.

## On the Road

After nearly four years I left Yunp'il Am. I believe now that had I stayed a further year I could have completed the task [full enlightenment]. However, I decided to go with a dharma friend who convinced me to travel with her. This friend was Pongong Sunim. She joined me because she had heard about my breakthrough and suggested we go to Mount Odae at the beginning of the free season. I agreed enthusiastically, thinking it would be a good place to practise and to complete the task.

Before leaving we performed a special session of chanting. For seven days we observed silence, chanted and remained standing throughout the day. At the end, a young boy appeared before me as if in a dream. Pongong Sunim did not see him, but I asked him where he had come from and why. He said he had come from Mount Odae and that the great Zen Master Hanam had told him to escort us there. This apparition was certainly a sign to strengthen our resolve.

So we left. On the way we took the opportunity to visit the Diamond Mountains. It was the first time I had seen such wonderful sights. At Podok Cave we performed another seven-day chanting session, then at Naksan Sa yet another, lasting 14 days. Towards the end of this chanting session the Bodhisattva Avalokitesvara, whose portrait was above the altar, appeared before me and said: 'If you are really intent on practice, why are you wandering idly about? Go quickly to meet the great Zen Master! Have a dharma exchange with him and practise hard!'

So we carried on towards Master Hanam's monastery. On penetrating the mountainous region around Mount Odae, we came to a small temple. As it was getting dark, we decided to stay the night. The three monks who occupied the temple were surprised to see us, as they were not used to encountering nuns who travelled for the sake of furthering their practice. As it was a small place, they partitioned off half the main room with a screen and insisted we sleep on the warmest part of the floor. It was the tenth month, snow was falling heavily and we were still 40 *li* [16 km/10 miles] from Master Hanam's monastery, Sangwon Sa.

The monks suggested we travelled via the Sinsollyong Pass, a route they thought would still be quite mild. After eating the rice they offered us, we left early. When we were midway up a mountain, suddenly a young man appeared and wanted to know where we were heading. After telling him, he advised us to sleep that night in a nearby village, as we were still far from our destination.

## Losing the Path

The following morning we set off again. It was a beautiful clear day, but at one stage we could not find the right path because of the snow. Only a few days remained before the meditation season began, yet here we were unable to either advance or retreat – it was most distressing. Then we heard a man shouting: 'What are you doing there? If you make a mistake now you may lose your way and freeze to death!' We begged him to point out the way and he told us to go by the middle path, but we could only just make it out. Curiously, he seemed to be the same person we had met the day before.

Eventually, dripping wet, we reached Sangwon Sa monastery. When we met Master Hanam, he was horrified to learn of the route we had taken in order to get there. Apparently even people who knew their way around those parts had frozen to death on the path we had taken. We told him how a young man had helped us. He commented that sometimes the Bodhisattva Manjusri revealed himself to the faithful when they were lost in the mountains.

After our interview, we discovered that five other nuns had arrived from Yunp'il Am. This made us very happy since there were 80 monks in residence.

After breakfast the following day, the seven of us went to bow formally to enter the assembly. The monks were very surprised to see seven nuns – the previous evening there had only been two – and they refused to accept us.

We were at a loss as to what to do next. Then Master Hanam kindly told us about Chijang Am, a nunnery 30 *li* [12 km/7½ miles] away, where we might be accepted for the meditation season. The abbess of Chijang Am turned out to be a dharma friend. She lived there with only one disciple and was glad to have us. On the first day of the meditation season, we had baths, shaved our heads and walked back to the monastery to listen to Master Hanam's lecture. This first lecture was about the *Platform Sutra* and I felt I could understand everything he said.

Master Hanam was most compassionate, almost mother-like in the way he endeavoured to make us understand and investigate. He knew that I had come from Master Mangong's place and was working on a *hwadu*, but I did not ask him about it when I first saw him. I never really did engage in dharma exchanges with him; my purpose in being there was purely to study under his direction, practise as hard as I could to awaken and then return to see Master Mangong.

## Temple Caretaker

Not long afterwards, an old nun asked if one of us would look after her small temple in the province of Kangnung. As it was the free season, I volunteered to go. The food there was very poor, as the old nun had locked the warehouse where the rice was stored before she went away, leaving me with only a meagre diet of potatoes and corn. I was not used to such food; until then I had always at least some rice to eat. Soon I began to feel dizzy. Then my whole body turned yellow with jaundice.

Some visiting nuns suggested I return to Chijang Am, but I would have rather died than to have failed in my duty. By now I had turned really yellow and, although I had no pain, I had no energy whatsoever. I could only eat the moku stalks which a younger dharma sister who had come to stay prepared and entreated me to eat. At least they had a sweet taste, which I enjoyed.

Then I had a dream. A young boy of 14 or so appeared before me with a shining bronze bowl filled with steaming sticky rice. He gave it to me and said that the inflammation due to malnutrition would be cured and I would recover. I ate it all and within three days my face regained its colour and my hunger disappeared. I felt now that I would live. Shortly after this the old nun came back and I returned to Chijang Am.

Upon my arrival I had another dream. Pongong Sunim and I were walking along a path when we met some children digging the ground. When I asked them what they were doing, they said they were extracting all kinds of medicines and gave us each a small piece. As I swallowed mine, I smelt a wonderful fragrance and my mind became peaceful and open. It was very refreshing and gave new strength to my faith. After that my health and appetite were completely restored.

I practised meditation as much as I could in Chijang Am. Nonetheless, I had to take care of many other things as well, which might have been a mistake at this point in my practice. Although I continually investigated the *hwadu* 'Return to the one', because the doubt had burst once before, I felt I knew the answer to the question. Consequently, this meant my doubt was not strong. So I kept holding the *hwadu* but without great inquiry. I should have asked Master Hanam about this, but I was thinking I would wait and ask Master Mangong.

## Uninhabited Temple

One day a friend and I got lost picking wild greens on the mountainside near Puktae. When we finally returned Pongong Sunim said she had prepared food for us at Puktae. So we went there, with the intention of visiting Sangwon Sa the next day to ask forgiveness for causing worry. Night had fallen by the time we arrived and it was very dark. Puktae was just an uninhabited temple, but because we were so full of sorrow at what had happened, we did not feel afraid. My dharma sister went straight to sleep but I just sat, unable to sleep because of the shame.

I felt nothing – no pain, no hunger – just the piercing sense of having made others unhappy. Yet by the middle of the night, my shame had transformed into a state of clarity and quiescence. My mind held no thoughts, just the *hwadu*. Suddenly there was a swishing sound and the candle blew out. My friend kept snoring. Had I been nervous I would have died at that moment, but I simply stood up, relit the candle and resumed the sitting. I reflected on a Zen Master called Naong who had lived in this place long ago and thought of the hardships he must have endured.

When we met Master Hanam the next day, I told him I had been unable to sleep and had meditated all night. He congratulated me on my practice and said we were only able to stay in Puktae because of my good meditation. 'That was a spirit who blew out your candle,' he said. 'It has been up there for three years now. A thief from a village in the valley went up one day and tried to steal rice from the monk who was practising there. The monk was killed in the ensuing fight. Because he fought with the thief, the monk became a spirit, which would not have happened had he died quietly with a virtuous mind.'

## Mangong Dies

Around this time I heard the sad news of Master Mangong's death. I cried a great deal. Master Mangong had been like a fierce and abrupt father. He would only listen to words of awakening and always tried to help people arouse the true mind. Sometimes he would write to meditators during the second half of the meditation season. Once he sent me a letter at Yunp'il Am, asking me to write to him with my questions. I wrote: 'After boiling a rock until it is soft, I will offer it to the good-knowing advisor.' He replied that he preferred his rock uncooked.

I was unable to attend either the funeral or the forty-ninth day death ceremony, but was determined to attend the hundredth-day ceremony. Afterwards, Pophui Sunim, senior advisor for the nuns at nearby Kyongsong Am, advised me not to return to Chijang Am. Moreover, the abbess of the nunnery emphasized how important it was for me to spend the coming season with a large assembly to meditate and attend to other duties. I argued that I had to go, since I had not brought a quilt and my backpack was empty. She said someone else could bring my things when they came this way. Since she insisted so much, I had no choice but to spend the summer at Kyongsong Am.

## Three-Year Term

At Kyongsong Am I was immediately given the job of food supervisor. Before completing the allotted period for this duty, however, I was asked to serve as kitchen assistant instead. It seemed they really did not want me to go away. I tried to refuse this job on the grounds that I did not know how to handle money, shop in the market or speak properly. I was told I would be given help and heard someone say impatiently: 'Who do these young people think they are, just wandering about from Zen hall to Zen hall without ever assuming any responsibilities? It won't do!' So I took on the position of kitchen assistant for the next three years and practised in the Zen hall whenever I had some time off.

I was meditating early one morning when I felt as though I had been struck by a thunderbolt and that a piece of the moon had entered me. My mind was very clear and my body felt as if it had blown away. I shouted: 'I am liberated from birth and death!' Everyone in the Zen hall was startled and no doubt wondered what kind of dream I had been having. So I left the room, chuckling to myself, and walked about quietly outside for a while.

Before the three years were up, I decided to leave. However, the night before I planned to make my three formal bows of departure in the main hall, Master Mangong appeared to me in a dream. He asked the celebrant to beat the wooden bell to call the kitchen assistant. For a deceased Zen Master to be concerned about a humble kitchen assistant made me think that I must have performed my duty badly. I put on my gown and formal robe, then entered his room to bow. He looked so alive that it did not feel like a dream at all.

As I was bowing, he said: 'I heard that you are quitting your duty.'

'Yes, I'm leaving,' I replied in a small voice.

He said: 'You must finish your full three years, only then will you conclude your task.'

But I insisted that I had made up my mind and would leave the next day. So that morning I did indeed make my formal bows to the assembly.

Shortly afterwards Kobong Sunim, the new Zen Master at Chonghye Sa, asked for me to see him. He told me: 'You have made a mistake. The community asked me to persuade you to complete the full three years of your responsibilities. If the community approves of something, then it is certain the Buddha approves of it. I heard about your experiences at Yunp'il Am and am convinced that if you stay the full three years at Kyongsong Am, you will finish your task.'

I replied that I had had enough and was going.

Later I had another dream which impressed upon me that if I completed the full three years at Kyongsong Am, I would complete all the meritorious actions necessary. But if I failed to complete these actions, then I would be unable to give dharma talks. (In fact, this turned out to be true. I have never been able to give dharma talks.) Despite these dreams and the entreaty of Kobong Sunim, I relinquished my post.

Pophui Sunim suggested that I rest from my years as kitchen assistant and invited me to accompany her to a nunnery she was to take care of near Seoul. I accepted gladly.

The nuns there wanted me to become the leader of the Zen hall. I tried to refuse on the grounds that I was too old and did not know how to do it. But they insisted: 'You should know how to do it. We've all heard of your experiences in Yunp'il Am.'

'I'm speechless,' I replied.

'If you're speechless, then I'll speak for you,' someone retorted. 'Just do it!'

So I spent the summer being the leader of the Zen hall.

## The Korean War and After

At the beginning of the free season, I told Pophui Sunim I had to visit my elder in Magok Sa for a short while. Although I arrived there without my backpack, due to the outbreak of the Korean War, it was three years before I could leave. The Communists had threatened to kill the great monks, so many of them, along with other practitioners, sought refuge in Magok Sa. It was said that the monastery was protected by the gods. And it was true; we were left completely untouched by the war.

After the war, Pongong Sunim came to Magok Sa and suggested we go to study together at Tonghwa Sa, a monastery near the city of Daegu, where Zen Master Hyobong was residing. I spent two years there.

I remember him giving a lecture in which he said: 'There is a high platform in the sky. Where should the Buddha stand?' I went and stood in front of him. He laughed and said I had understood.

On another occasion, Master Hyobong received some leaves in an envelope from Master Kyongbong. He asked us the meaning of this. I said: 'He had already got it wrong when he picked the leaves.'

Master Hyobong was very compassionate, always trying to help people investigate and understand. My practice went well while listening to his lectures.

After leaving Tonghwa Sa, Pongong Sunim and I wandered for three years, meditating here and there. We ended up in the city of Namhae, where there is a special temple that Zen nuns and monks use to perform chanting sessions. We stayed in a little hermitage nearby which had been built by a laywoman. We would go to Namhae for seven days of chanting and then come back to the hermitage to practise meditation. I stayed there for three years, but only performed the chanting sessions during the first season.

Towards the end of the Korean War I had taken charge of my first disciple. A monk had brought her to the temple and told her to bow to the nun she would like to have as her teacher. She bowed to me. Since she was already quite old, I was afraid she would not be able to study the sutras well because of the need to memorize so many texts. So after two years, I sent her to Zen halls where there were good Zen nun masters, such as Pophui Sunim and Mansong Sunim. She especially liked Mansong Sunim.

I did not see my disciple for a long time, then one day she showed up at the hermitage. She said I had become thin and that my clothes were very poor, and encouraged me to return with her to Taesong Am, the nunnery of Mansong Sunim. Although Pongong Sunim was annoyed that I should pay heed to my disciple, her suggestion actually corresponded with my own wishes. So I decided to go, Pongong Sunim promising to join us later.

Mansong Sunim took great care of me and provided me with medicines which helped my face become quite full.

Once Mansong Sunim and I went to the river bank. She asked: 'Is it the river that flows or the wind that blows?'

I replied: 'It is your mind that flows.'

She laughed.

This is the only time we ever had a dharma exchange.

## Settling Down

Then we went together to Naewon Sa to help with a special death ceremony. Mansong Sunim wanted to take me back with her, but the nuns in Naewon Sa asked me to stay on as their senior advisor. By becoming a permanent resident I would be able to take care of the young Zen nuns who came to practise. Until then, it was the custom for nuns only to stay for the meditation seasons, leaving the place rather empty in between. The abbess, Suok Sunim, begged me to consider the nunnery as my home, thereby encouraging nuns to live there all year round.

I greatly enjoyed staying in Naewon Sa and became very enthusiastic. The two masters who visited regularly, Master Hyanggok and Master Kyongbong, inspired me greatly. This was especially helpful since my determination had weakened considerably after the death of Master Mangong. Working on the *hwadu* 'Return to the one' I understood that everything returns to the one and the one returns to the midst of the mind and finishes there. After listening to Master Hyanggok, however, I adopted the *hwadu* 'No!' and have practised that ever since.

Master Kyongbong once wrote on a piece of paper: 'Where do all the sutras come from? Where did the Buddha get them from?'

I asked him: 'Why, great monk, do you bother with distracted thoughts like that?'

He nodded and laughed.

Although Master Kyongbong was kind, I did not feel strongly inclined to discuss my practice with him. Perhaps it was because he was so old and frail and would leave immediately after his talks.

Master Hyanggok, on the other hand, was strong and rough – indeed, quite frightening. I remember him shouting at us once: 'You are here in great numbers, but what are you doing?

Eating food, taking care of yourselves, sightseeing, just gobbling up the rice of the laity? Why are you playing around all day? Why don't you practise?'

Then he gave a talk. Just before the end he shouted: 'Ten thousand Manjusris are here. Find the true and original one!' and stormed off to his room.

I ran after him in my formal robes, shouting: 'The true Manjusri, the Buddhas of the three periods, the patriarchs of the lineage, the masters of the present age, they all come out of my nostrils!'

He laughed and asked: 'Where are your nostrils?'

I answered: 'Originally there are no nostrils, but as I cannot speak without saying something, I said it in this way.'

He laughed again and said: 'You put much effort into your practice. Make the young nuns practise well and guide them.'

Shortly after this encounter he died. He had given this lecture because he knew he did not have long to live.

I entered the Zen hall when I was 32 and have grown old in it. When I was younger, the practice was so urgent, I barely had the time to eat. If I had worked the full three years that time in Kyongsong Am, I'm sure I could have finished the task. But when I listen to the dharma talks of great monks, I realize there are many things I know, and just as many I do not.

# 3
## the glass is already broken
### Ayya Khema

Ayya Khema was a Buddhist nun who lived in Germany and
taught world-wide. A homely woman who raised a family,
she exuded a refreshing directness, and her occasional severity
was tempered by genuine warmth and kindness. A leading
Buddhist figure in Europe, she was the author of *Being Nobody,
Going Nowhere* (Wisdom, 1987). She died of cancer in 1997.

## Living or Dying

When I was told recently I had breast cancer and needed treatment it was not news to me. I had known it for 10 years and had spent this time living with the cancer, using my time fruitfully so that when it was no longer manageable I would be ready to die. I had done nothing about the cancer, taken no chemotherapy or drugs, as I had not wanted to get caught in the medical trap of pills and check ups.

I thought that if I was going to die, so be it; if I was going to live, so be it. But the point came where I could no longer live with the constant discomfort. It took nine years for the pain to start, but it became so bad that I had to take painkillers and I felt this was not useful.

I finally accepted that I needed an operation and now I only have to take one hormone pill a day. The doctors and nurses were extremely kind to me and the whole experience of being in hospital was most interesting. The nurses asked questions about the dharma and I had a wonderful time. I also had an excellent rest which I needed badly, as I was quite run down with waiting so long. I spent five weeks in hospital and four weeks in a sanatorium.

My life has changed since then. I continue my work of spreading the dharma as I did before, but I have experienced a complete letting go and freedom from wanting. There were days in hospital, especially two which I will not forget, when I felt the end was near, as my whole energy was dissipating. I could hardly talk and it seemed as if my faculties were leaving me. I had no objection, but the doctors and nurses did everything they could to keep me alive. I decided that if they were trying so hard, maybe I should try a little too, so I did.

Also, my students, friends and supporters sent me cards and flowers; some telephoned me. Many told me it did not matter whether I continued teaching, but knowing I was there was important. This encouraged me to try a little harder to be there for them.

Now for me, 'the glass is already broken'. Once a Westerner asked Achaan Chah, a great Thai teacher, why he had so many material things in his room. He replied: 'You see this glass, to me it is already broken. While it is still intact on the table I use it. It even has beautiful colours when the sun shines and a lovely sound when I hit it with a spoon. But for me, it is already broken.' This means no attachment, not trying to keep anything.

## Illness Can Be a Great Teacher

If you are practising Buddhism already, there is no doubt that you can use illness as a great teacher, because it is typical *dukkha* [suffering]. When the Buddha was still a Bodhisattva and not yet enlightened, he saw an old person, a sick person and a dead person. Through these experiences he recognized transiency and suffering, which caused him to search for the answer to human pain and grief. Some people must experience *dukkha* before they start to practise and sometimes illness can help to start a spiritual journey. If you are already on a spiritual journey, there is no doubt that illness is an experience in letting go. We realize this is part of ordinary, universal human suffering.

In hospital we only see sick people, doctors and nurses, and medicines. We realize there are hundreds of patients in one hospital and each country has hundreds of hospitals. This helps us see what our priorities are, because if we are seriously ill, death becomes a reality. This provides a wonderful opportunity to let go of everything. We can actually experience losing all sense of personality and individuality; they dissolve into the primordial ground of being, from which everything arises.

If we do not die, but stay alive, it is a bonus, and we can use this near death experience. We can consider ourselves as already dead, but having been given a little extra time to help others. Imagining ourselves already dead means we no longer look for personal results or gain. If we are already dead, what can we gain? We can, however, use the extra time given to us fruitfully; in my case, spreading the dharma.

I have learned concentration through meditation. Since I have been practising for 30 years my meditation has reached the point where I do not have to use any methods, I can just sit down and concentrate. After 30 years, I would hope so! I am not distracted by noise or external disturbances. This has developed over the last eight or nine years of practice. However, concentration is one thing, insight is another. Letting go of life expectancy makes all the difference.

## Guidance for Beginners

In learning concentration complete beginners might find it easier to watch their breath with an aid. If they like numbers, they can count their breaths. If they like words, they can use words like 'love' or 'peace'. If they are visually inclined, they can use an ocean wave. Visualizing the breath as an ocean wave, coming in and out, can help concentration, as can breathing in 'love' and out 'peace'.

Once people are a little more concentrated, they can follow the beginning, middle and end of each breath, or follow the sensations accompanying it. They can rest their awareness on the numerous sensations between nostrils and abdomen.

Then I would lead into impermanence by seeing the impermanence of the breath and thoughts. If you label your disrupting thoughts, you will get an idea of your habitual thought patterns. We use one descriptive word such as 'future', 'past', 'planning', 'remembering', 'wanting', 'rejecting', 'resisting', 'bored', 'disinterest', 'nonsense', 'fantasy', 'dream'. It does not matter which word comes to mind first. Eventually you can see a pattern, for example that you are constantly planning. When you notice your thought patterns in this way, you can see they are non-productive and drop them.

## The Observer Is Not the Thinker

The other great benefit from labelling is experiencing that the observer is not the thinker. We can use this in daily life by substituting the unwholesome with the wholesome in the same way we substitute thoughts with attention on the breath in meditation. The Buddha called this 'substituting the four supreme efforts', namely not allowing unwholesome thoughts to remain, but exchanging them with their opposite. This is one of the main purification practices. In order to practise this, we have to know the contents of our minds.

Labelling is for beginners. For someone who is concentrated and has only an occasional thought, it would not be useful, but for the beginner it is extremely helpful. It also brings the benefit of seeing that thoughts need not be believed; they are just thoughts. There is no need to act upon them. If we can see that, we stop arguing, which is a pleasant change.

## In Everyday Life

In everyday life, mindfulness is very important. Mindfulness in Buddhist teachings is coupled with clear comprehension; they belong together. Clear comprehension means that you inquire into your purposes and motivation and see whether you are using skilful means. We also cultivate purification of heart and mind, making sure we do not retain negative thoughts and emotions, constantly exchanging them with positive thoughts and emotions. This substituting of opposites, together with mindfulness, purifies us automatically.

Then there is daily meditation. This is as important as daily eating. It can be beneficial to join or start a group which gives support so you do not feel entirely alone. If you are interested in the Buddhist teachings from the Pali Canon, I would recommend the books of the Buddhist Publication Society of Kandy, Sri Lanka. The Buddha taught *Pariyatti pati patti: pariyatti* means 'study', *pati-patti* means 'practice', and they must go together.

## The Understood Experience

We must understand our experiences on all levels. If we do not understand them, what good are they to us? One woman of 60 came to see me and told me she had had an experience 30 years ago which she had never forgotten, but could not understand. She had entered the fifth *jhana* [meditative absorption] spontaneously.

After we discussed her experience, she could at last relate to it meaningfully, gain insight from it and enter the path of meditation. If she had known to look it up in the Buddha's teachings, she might have understood earlier. The experiences we have are in our hearts, that is our feelings; understanding is in our minds. The two work together to make a whole.

## The *Jhanas*

My main meditation practice is the *jhanas*. This is practising concentration [samatha]. The higher *jhanas* – fifth, sixth, seventh – are called vipassana-*jhanas*. They bring automatic insight into the non-existing self which helps us let go of the illusion of an inherently existing self. How to let go is expounded on in detail by the Buddha and is found in the *Discourses of the Middle Length Sayings* (*Majjhima Nikaya*).

The three higher *jhanas* are called 'infinity of space', 'infinity of consciousness' and 'the base of nothingness'. If we truly experience them, we know we are not here, that we have made the 'I' up in our minds. Then we can actually try letting go of this illusion. Non-attachment and discernment are the path which the Buddha prescribed and practised.

Altogether there are eight *jhanas*. The first could be translated as 'rapture and bliss'; this does not really say much about it, but it is the most exquisite sensation. The first four are called *rupa-jhanas*, meaning 'fine-material-absorptions'. The next four are the *arupa-jhanas*, which are the 'formless' absorptions. The first four provide experiential insight if we use them correctly and have authentic guidance. We have to give up self and self-concern on different levels in order to gain concentration, which then brings clear understanding.

The fifth, sixth and seventh *jhanas* provide definite insights into this illusory self, which facilitates giving up self-illusion. At the end of working with the *jhanas*, I teach and practise to see whether our minds are actually willing to let go of self-cherishing and can experience the unconditioned. There are certain ways of doing this and it is not as impossible as it may sound.

I generally teach the *jhanas* to people who are no longer beginners, but there are people in a meditation course who have not meditated before who can benefit from this teaching. My teacher has said that this depends on our past lives. If we have practised in past lives, we can do them, otherwise we can start now.

## 'All the World's a Stage'

The idea that the *jhanas* are dangerous because people could grasp at the blissful experiences is an old chestnut. Firstly, if we grasp something, we have not realized it. Secondly, real insight comes with real calm. We cannot have a little of this and a lot of the other. A little bit of calm brings only a little bit of insight.

The interesting point is that anybody who has been meditating can practise the *jhanas*. Then meditation becomes something that has substance and is fulfilling. We realize that there is more to the world than what we see and this makes all the difference to our inner lives.

The Buddha continued meditation after his enlightenment. On his deathbed, he went up to the eighth *jhana*, down towards the first and died between the fourth and fifth. This is related by the Venerable Anuruddha, who had psychic abilities, in the *Paranibbana Sutra*, which tells about the Buddha's death.

The Buddha said you can have an experience of the unconditioned after realizing any of the *jhanas*. It is, however, unlikely this would happen after realizing the first *jhana*, because it does not usually give enough insight. After attaining the *jhanas*, experiencing complete calm and an altered consciousness, then is the time to direct the mind towards the unconditioned.

Whether you can do this or not depends on how completely you can give up and let go. This instruction to direct the mind towards the unconditioned is for anyone who has mastered the *jhanas*. Mastering the *jhanas* means one can enter at will, stay for any length of time, review each step afterwards and also jump from any *jhana* to any other. This has always been considered very difficult. It is quite amazing, however, how many people, with some concentration and ability, can practise the *jhanas*.

With the help of the *jhanas* we can see the world in a different way. Our meditation feels different and our whole outlook on the world changes, even without an enlightenment experience. It is like Shakespeare said: 'All the world's a stage and all the men and women merely players.'

However, because we are alive we continue the play. A person who sees the world as a stage and has understood the Buddha's teaching will teach and reach out to the world out of compassion. What else could one do?

## How I Did It Myself

In 1963 I spent a few months at the Sri Aurobindo ashram in Pondicherry. Sri Aurobindo was dead, but the Mother was still alive and she was teaching meditation. We would sit under the stars on the playground of the school and listen to her. This was my first introduction to meditation and I liked it right away.

What was missing for me were exact guidelines. I always thought it was wonderful if a sage was enlightened, but how could I do it myself? I tried to find a path. I read the books of the Mother, which are pragmatic and realistic, but I could not fathom her teacher, Sri Aurobindo.

In 1973 the Venerable Khantipalo, an English Buddhist monk, came to Australia and with him my first introduction to the Buddha's teaching. Here was a pathway I could understand and practise, and I felt it was the right spiritual approach for me.

I started studying the Buddha's teachings as they were transmitted to us in the Pali Canon, translated into English. I found guidelines which were pragmatic and realistic, everyday kind of things that I could get my teeth into. As I learned about the five hindrances I tried to practise getting rid of them. It was fascinating. After about three years the Venerable Khantipalo asked me to teach with him.

Every time I read a sutra I try to put it into practice. I am still reading the sutras because there are so many and I find new ones all the time. I frequently teach according to the sutras. If you are not already practising Buddhist meditation the sutras may be quite difficult to understand; we cannot read a sutra as if it were an ordinary book.

## The Best Thing I Ever Did!

I became a nun in 1979. I had established Wat Buddha Dhamma in Australia and was teaching with Phra Khantipalo. I thought the only sensible thing to do was to become a nun. It was the only way to be protected from all the worldly things which take so much time and effort. I had done many things already and I had worked for the Bank of America for seven years. But who wants to do this all one's life?

To be a nun is a big advantage for me. I do not have to look after a car, or drive. I do not have a bank account to balance. I do not have to shop and buy food, look after a hairdo or buy clothes. I do not even have to answer the telephone.

It is absolute protection for the person and an enormous advantage for practice. Almost immediately after becoming a nun I got this wonderful liberating feeling: 'I do not have to be anybody. I do not have to be beautiful, attractive, interesting or rich. I can just put on these robes and do the best I can.'

It was a real feeling of release, an absolute relief. Once you shave off your hair and put on robes you are yourself without pretence. You are just a person in robes. If someone likes you, that is fine; if not, that does not matter either. It is the best thing I ever did!

## Helping the Nun Movement

In Sri Lanka I established a Pappuduwa nuns' island, next to the monks' island which the Venerable Nyanyatiloka had established in 1911, in the same Radgania Lake. I was able to do that because I had a dedicated supporter who was living right on the edge of the lake. I felt I could trust this man completely, so I gave him all the donations I received and he had a nunnery built on the island. Many Western women came to the island to practise or ordain. Two of my nuns are there now, running the nunnery and teaching.

My friend Ayya Nyanyasiri, an American nun in Sri Lanka, has organized a place where the nuns give talks and do pujas. The status of nuns in Sri Lanka is pretty low, but due to such efforts it is improving. Now the government is trying hard to uplift their educational level. Two of my meditation students are teaching meditation to nuns at this time.

In 1987, I took full ordination at Hsi Lai Temple in Los Angeles. I did this to be in accord with other Western nuns, who had become bhikkhunis. It did not change my life or my work in any way, but it was a most interesting experience and I am glad I went through with it.

At this point I am happy to help the international Buddhist women's movement. It is important that women in the different world religions take on more responsibilities, but under no circumstances should there be any animosity towards men. I do not think the Buddhist women I am associated with are guilty of that duality.

Religion is the last stronghold of a patriarchal system where women find it difficult to develop their potential. On the other hand, I must say that any great woman has always been able to make her mark.

In 1987 I was invited to a Buddhist–Christian dialogue at the University of California in Berkeley. We had a panel of women consisting of two Buddhists and two Christians. The Christians spoke first about the problems inherent in 'women and religion'. When my turn came I said I was delighted to see that my Christian sisters were having as much trouble as we were. I brought the house down with laughter, but I meant it quite seriously. There were 700 listeners who all seemed very sympathetic and supportive.

There were 12 evenings with one lecture. Eleven were given by men and only one by women. All the men spoke for an hour; we were four women and only had 15 minutes each. We told the organizer: 'You were lucky to get four for the price of one!' This was in 1987 at the University of California in America, which is supposed to be the most liberated country in regard to sexism. But it was done totally unwittingly, without any ill intention.

## Tradition Is Not Orthodoxy

When I found the Buddha's teachings to follow I was absolutely delighted. I use this tradition to foster my own practice and understanding, and I could not do it without the Buddha's guidelines. When I teach, I explain the essence according to my own experience, without deviating from the basic framework laid down by the Buddha, though I might add my own interpretations of traditional formulas.

I have found a wealth of instructions in the Pali Canon which I try to transmit through my own experiences and understanding. For years I discussed my ideas with, and had them confirmed by, my teacher, who was totally traditional. The Venerable Naññarama became my teacher about 14 years ago when I was looking for someone to discuss and confirm my jhanic experiences. I had asked other teachers about this, but they were not very helpful. The Venerable Naññarama died at the beginning of 1992 at the age of 91. He was a great support to me. Checking experiences and insights with him over and over again, I could be sure I was not imagining them or interpreting them wrongly.

The Venerable Naññarama instructed me to go out and teach the *jhanas* because they were becoming a lost art. I was hesitant at first, but I found that many people could do them and it made a great difference in their lives.

I am traditional, but certainly not orthodox, because I find orthodoxy binding, not liberating. I am Jewish and find Orthodox Judaism can imprison people in unsuitable behaviour, such as wearing fur caps in a hot climate. The same dangers are inherent in the orthodoxy of the Theravada tradition.

Tradition can be relieving and releasing because we know it is based on absolute truths which have stood the test of time. Thus tradition should be kept and followed. Orthodoxy I see as narrowly following a certain behaviour pattern no longer appropriate in a different country at a different time. I would like to modify the behaviour pattern to adapt to the society we live in, so that it does not present difficulties for ordinary people.

## Is Buddhism Socially Acceptable?

Buddhism in the West must stop expressing itself in the foreign languages of Asia and speak modern Western languages. There is a discourse by the Buddha called *The Exposition of Non-Conflict* in which he explains that the dharma has to be learned in one's mother tongue and taught in a precise manner. However, the essence of the teaching must not be watered down. When we try to cater to people's ideas and look for social acceptance we lose the grandeur and splendour of a totally liberating ideal.

Society's aim is getting, becoming, having and retaining. Liberation is the path of letting go, not becoming; just being and renunciation. It is the exact opposite of what society usually wants. Diluted Buddhism pandering to society's desires becomes psychodharma which contains only partial truths. Buddhist practice is a total turn-about of one's inner being, not just improving one's behaviour and reactions. In the West, this tendency of diluting the dharma endangers its authenticity.

We have to make sure that the dharma is taught for one reason only, namely the attainment of Nirvana. This is our reason for practising, for teaching, for meditating in the Buddha's way. It is important to keep this in mind as an overall direction. If Nirvana is no longer sought, then the dharma becomes either psychology or philosophy, or even membership of a club of like-minded people.

## Nirvana

Nirvana is the complete loss of any feeling of personal identity. Actually it is much easier to be in the world without personal identity. If one is very fat and wants to go through a door, one will hit the doorframe on both sides, which is painful. In the same way if one has a fat ego, one will hit obstructions every-where, which is hurtful all the time. If there is no ego left, noth-ing hurts.

We function much better without ego. Life becomes an inter-esting stage play with some nice backdrops. In the *Mahamangala Sutra* it says: 'Although touched by worldly circumstances, the enlightened one's mind is never wavering.' Being touched by worldly circumstances, the mind does not move with them. The complete loss of ego is enlightenment, but the way is composed of many stages of loss, till we are finally rid of the whole illu-sory dream.

We can utilize the teachings of the Buddha and realize them, whether we belong to a religious tradition or not. Contradictions are human; in reality there is only one truth and mystics of all ages have always found the same truth. There is universal con-sciousness and that can be experienced in meditation – the infinity of consciousness.

Every mind that meditates eventually goes along the same path, because there is no other path. Whether we call ourselves Christian, Muslim, Jew or Buddhist does not matter, we all have a human mind. Religious intolerance is as absurd as our ego-centricity.

Universal consciousness is not Buddhist, but infinite. The infinity of space is not Buddhist, but just infinity. Infinity of con-sciousness is the cause for the experience of the base of nothing-ness into which everything dissolves.

## A Compassionate Response

After a retreat people sometimes are bothered by all the impuri-ties in the environment. The only cure is loving-kindness and compassion – to respond with compassion everywhere, wherever one finds oneself. Every instance when we meet somebody can be considered a challenge to our practice.

In retreats we do loving-kindness meditation every evening as a group. It helps to become familiar and intimate with this feeling. All of us have many confrontations with other people, so one of the most important things we can do is to practise loving-kindness. Sitting silently in meditation is only one method. We cannot sit in front of somebody and say, 'Wait a minute, I have got to sit before I can be kind to you!' Compassion is something we can familiarize ourselves with day after day till it becomes a natural response.

# 4
## the ABC of meditation
### Aoyama Sensei

Aoyama Sensei is the abbess of a large training centre for nuns of the Soto Zen tradition in Japan. She is a renowned writer and expert in the art of tea and flower arrangement. She is formal yet simple and has a commanding presence softened by great kindness.

## Sit Straight and Be Straight

The ABC of zazen [*za*, 'sitting', *zen*, 'meditation'] is to regulate the body; that is, to cross the legs, put the hands together, straighten the back. Straightening the back means your rear end is out, your belly is out on the other side and your back is in. Then you regulate the breath. Regulating the body and regulating the spirit are not separate; the spiritual form is symbolized by this physical form.

Do not lean one way or the other, either to the left or to the right. Keep straight. If your zazen is going well, there is a tendency to become arrogant and to feel on top of the world. If things are not going well, you can get depressed, but it is important not to go either way and to remain central. Sit straight and be straight in the practice.

The final step for developing the correct posture is harmonizing your breathing with your posture. Start by breathing out, expelling all your breath and letting your body follow this, then let the breath come in gradually while you correct your posture. As you breathe out, you expel all the bad chi [energy]. As you release all the stale air which has built up in your lungs, you also expel all extraneous thoughts and wandering fantasies.

As you breathe out, your organs relax. If there is tension your organs might feel agitated and if you sit with this tension, you will end up feeling rather bad. Once you breathe this tension out, feeling empty, your posture is ready.

## Reflections in a Mirror

Now you are breathing well and your body is in the right position. Everything is in balance, but you must remember this is connected with the spirit. Even when everything is settled and your mind is receptive to harmony, ideas occur. You hear things. A change in the light registers in your eyes. These are natural functions of the mind and should not be rejected, but you must not pursue them either. They are like reflections in a mirror.

The thoughts that arise are like the first arrow. It is important not to grasp and follow the thoughts, which are like the second and third arrows. Let the first arrow fall without following the thoughts. If you hear a car outside, do not start to think: 'Where is that man going so quickly?' If a thought arises, do not pursue it, because at this point it starts to become attachment and passion.

The idea that arises is usually the master in the sense that we tend to follow after it like a slave. Zazen practice is not letting the idea become the master. Do not follow it, let it go. If ideas come up, just return to your sitting straight away. I like to use a Christian example. Zazen is like the cross. Christ on the cross is the symbol of the death of the ordinary ego. The self dies to the self and is reborn as the universal.

We often think that our ideas are wonderful things, but they have been here 20, 30, 50 or maybe 100 years already. What a human being can think about and understand is really quite limited, and is generally ego-centred. Very few ideas are worth following anyway.

We sit, expecting this self which chases after ideas and things is meeting its end, yet stray thoughts come up again and again. Every time we realize that we have been riding a train of thoughts back to England or off to America, we must return to our sitting. We must awaken the desire for enlightenment. Billions of times we may realize we have wandered off, but all we need do is return to our bodhi-minds [awakening minds] and our sitting.

Zazen becomes the foundation, and the process of regulating your body, breathing and mind; not chasing after stray thoughts, returning always to the matter at hand, just sitting.

This becomes the foundation on which you cultivate this outlook, this spirit, bringing it into your inner life.

When you are cleaning, keep your posture and mind on the cleaning. Whatever you do, keep your mind on the matter at hand and return to it at once if you stray. Your whole life has to become a place of practice. Kodo Sawaki said: 'Religion is life.' This is our everyday life – cleaning, washing up, just doing our jobs. Religion has to come to life, into everyday life.

## Beggars' Zen

Do not try to gain something through religious training. Of course a person who has undergone training will be different, but this is just the result, not the goal to aim for. Training with the intention of gaining something for yourself is beggars' Zen.

The character for training in Japanese is *shugyo*. There are two ways of writing *shu*. One is with the character also used in big business. It involves a certain job and attaining a certain skill or ability, like a doctor, for example. The other way is to give yourself to something. Religion, *gyo*, is to move, to do. It is something you do, not something for developing a certain skill. People who pursue meditation with the intention that it is going to lead to something or gain something for themselves often drop off after a number of years.

## Wisdom and Compassion

Though training is an essential foundation for a life of practice, you could sit zazen with the wrong spirit. After a number of years it changes your personality, so the training has to be correct. You find out if it is correct by listening to a teacher you respect and by reading Buddhist writings. This is wisdom.

The world of wisdom is the world of intellect. Compassion is the world of feeling. We must remember that feeling is stronger than intellect. We might know that some action is not good, but feel unable to stop; for example, people carry on smoking, knowing it is bad for their health.

Compassion involves love, but the root of compassion is knowing we suffer together. The Buddha suffered together with all living beings. This is why he understood all our pain and desires. If you understand and deepen this, the energy of feeling will penetrate and enthuse your training. Again, it must go in the right direction, that is the function of wisdom.

## The Source of Our Misery

Compassion comes from a world view in which all life is seen simply as an expression of underlying universal unity. However, our own little egos do not realize our existence emerges from a universal light source. The little ego does not want to get hurt, it wants good things for itself, and wanting to protect the little ego is the source of all our pains. As long as we do not realize this is the source of our misery, there is no possibility of overcoming it.

This room is brightly lit and looks clean, but if you make it dark and channel the light, you can see the dust very clearly in the shaft of light. Through hearing Buddhist teachings we can see our own faults and where they are coming from. We realize what a sorry state we are in.

Through this understanding and the tears that come from it, we can look at other people who are suffering and are only pre-occupied with their own selves without getting angry at them. We can sympathize with them, feeling compassion. This is the beginning of genuine compassion; suffering together with others instead of criticizing and denouncing them.

Practising wisdom alone is not enough and if you are not moved by compassion, your training is shallow. Suffering together with people is the real training. When the other person sees you are not condemning them and you are suffering with them, or that you are suffering because of them, they will feel very differently. You may become truly awakened through finally understanding another person.

# 5

## serenity and stillness
## Maechee Pathomwan

Maechee Pathomwan is the head nun for a whole province in Thailand. She is tall and thin, wears white robes, and looks pure and peaceful. But the stories about her childhood in the temple can be quite funny and mischievous. She has been a nun for 38 years and has been teaching vipassana [understanding of the central truths of the dharma by means of meditation practice] for many years.

# Ghosts and Snakes

I was ordained as a nun when I was 12 years old. I had been inspired to join the order since I was very young and when I was seven I asked my father if I could take up the robes. He allowed me to go when I was 12 for a week only, but I kept extending the deadline week by week.

When I was younger I noticed that although the worldly life was quite happy and fine, there was something special about the ordained people I came in contact with. They had this serenity about them, a stillness, and that attracted me. At first I just wanted to try it for a week, like I promised my father.

The first week I was taught the morning and evening chanting. I saw people practising and I wanted to get involved in it. I learned the meditation where you notice the breath in the abdomen. You become aware that your chest fills with air, your abdomen expands, then you exhale and it is empty. I wanted to see what the outcome of practising this would be.

Five years later, after graduating from the dharma study school, I moved to Nanachat, a monastery where I learned the four foundations of mindfulness as the basis for meditation. After meeting Ajahn Dhammadaro, the abbot, I decided that if I could teach I would stay a nun all my life.

As a young nun I was very afraid of ghosts, so I went to stay in a small *kuti* [hut] by the charnel ground. I was gripped by a paralysing fear several times, but I decided to remain meditating to overcome the fear.

Another time someone had carved a watermelon and put a candle in it and seeing this I feared it was a ghost. However, before running away, I stopped and stood still, looking clearly at that ghost, as my father had suggested, till I realized it was a watermelon with a candle.

The temple where I was staying was famous for being infested by snakes. One day I decided to stay still for three hours, but after 10 minutes I felt something cold on my leg. I was afraid it was a ghost and I opened my eyes. I was relieved to see it was only a poisonous snake, so I sat even stiller, as recommended by my teacher when encountering snakes.

From my teacher I learned the 'lifting of the palm' meditation. First for three days and three nights I lifted and lowered the palm of my hand until I felt the consciousness in the palm of my hand. Then I practised 12 days consecutively to see what would happen. Finally I went into a six-month solitary retreat.

Once I decided to sit for three hours watching the rising and falling of the abdomen. I was very concentrated and felt very light and rapturous. Another nun was looking after me. When I opened my eyes after what seemed like 10 minutes and asked if the three hours were up, the other nun said that I had been sitting for 18 hours.

## Transformation

There has been a noticeable change in my personality during the course of my life. When I was younger, I was very hot-headed. I used to speak coarse language when I was angry and hit things. As I practised, that ceased, and there was more refinement and stillness. This is the main thing that has happened to me: developing the ability to watch anger as it arises and ceases with mindfulness and clear comprehension of its causes, and being able to deal with it without having to project it out. I feel that mindfulness, awareness and clear comprehension are very important in my daily life.

I started by having faith in Buddhism and the three jewels [Buddha, dharma, sangha]. The inspiration to enter the monastic life was based on the three refuges [Buddha, dharma and sangha]. As my practice grew it became more than an inspiration, because I saw how by practising with awareness I actually experienced things arising and ceasing. This continues to nurture my faith in Buddhism and in this way of life.

Realizing the fruits of the practice expands and stabilizes my faith in Buddhism. In one way my faith is constant, in another way I have more and more of it. I have more faith in the practice, in the belief that one can attain Nirvana through practising.

## Handlifting Meditation

To start meditating we could become aware of the tip of the nose, of the feeling of the breath passing through the nose as a point to focus on. Human beings are like cars – we need an exhaust pipe to get rid of our negativity and the suffering we bear. When we learn to breathe in to calm ourselves and to breathe out the negativities we are carrying around, it is like the car getting rid of carbon monoxide so it can continue to run.

Sometimes beginners come with strong emotions. If someone is angry, I try to make them breathe for three minutes. Once the practitioner sees the result of decreasing the anger, becoming calm, then they usually do it for five to ten minutes. Gradually I increase the time until they can really feel the benefit of meditation and then they generally ask me if they can sit longer.

By doing meditation handlifting, rising and falling, we realize the body and mind are connected. The mind is like the master, the body is like the servant. To be able to understand how we work, we must understand both mind and body. We focus on the hand because it is the hand that does the action. It is with the hand we commit bad or good deeds. Realizing and focusing the feeling within the hand, the consciousness within the hand, provide a way to watch the mind in connection with the body.

We might feel embarrassed sitting and lifting the hand repeatedly, but we do not have to do it around other people, we can do it on our own. After a while we might feel the hand pulsating like the heart. If we bring the awareness to a refined state we can actually feel the blood flow. It becomes another organ we can watch like breathing.

## Citta: Heart/Mind

After we have developed a strong foundation, we can sustain mindfulness for a long time and begin to watch the heart/mind [citta] directly. We can watch the reactions and feelings that arise. How does each feeling feel? What are we feeling at the moment of sitting? We try to be aware of the current feeling.

Citta is the centre of sensory perceptions and sensory consciousness. We have to focus on understanding how the sense organs contact the heart.

Because the heart is the centre of sensory consciousness, it is also the centre of defilements. It is the place where we can watch desire arise and grasping happen. We have to be able to sustain mindfulness in order to use it to comprehend each feeling as it arises. Then we go beyond the perception of it and understand the cause.

Once we realize defilements happen and we have a place, a centre, where perception, consciousness, feeling and volition happen, then we can practise in a way to watch them cease. Once we know how things are, once we know there is desire, we understand it, we do not grasp it anymore and then it ceases.

By practising in this way we can watch the arising and ceasing of things, and allow this movement to be as it is. We can see that the root cause of grasping and becoming has to do with anger, greed, lust and hatred. We can notice a certain feeling coming and making contact, and through that very awareness we disengage from it and it ceases.

When we see these feelings clearly, they dissolve. As we see desire happening and ceasing, we can decrease the actual process of grasping as we become more advanced in this technique. Automatically we start to reflect on *anicca* [impermanence], *dukkha* [suffering] and *anatta* [no-self ]; how things rise, how suffering comes in the course of life and how it ceases.

We continue to practise in this way; as things come, we watch them, we let them be around until we are able to comprehend exactly how they arose and then take them to cessation. Then we understand the first noble truth [suffering], the second [the cause of suffering], the third [the end of suffering] and the fourth [the path to end the suffering].

## Sensuality

We have to be careful about sensuality. When we lust after beautiful, sensual things, it is easy to be taken in by pleasure and either grasp the object or the pleasure created by it. It is important to watch our minds diligently. Be careful not to engage with pleasure, nor be in a situation or atmosphere where anger, hatred and other powerful emotions can arise.

It is easy to be carried away by delusion, not knowing what delusion actually means. Delusion is also like intoxication – the state of being intoxicated, not with external intoxicants, but more the moods and feelings we might have like love and lust, feelings we are addicted to, sensations that we chase. It is important to watch what makes us feel and what makes us lust after something.

## A Cool Space

I encourage laypeople to learn dana [giving], not so much materially giving external things to each other, but spiritual giving, like forgiving each other. You have to learn how to forgive your partner and allow them a certain space to go through what they have to go through.

When you are angry at your partner, it is important to find a space to balance out the negativity with positivity by recollecting the goodness this person has brought to you. Try not to grasp the moment of anger; instead try to find a cool space and balance it. See the loving kindness you can bring that person by balancing and encouraging yourself to feel *metta* [loving-kindness] towards your partner. It is important to know how to deal with problematic situations and thereby create harmony within the family.

I teach householders to look at the cause of *dukkha* in daily life and to see that often it is not external. It does not have to do with anyone in particular when you feel angry, upset or disappointed. It is usually yourself who feeds these emotions; the root cause is within. Be aware of speech and bodily actions. Calm down, understand that the cause of suffering is actually the feeling, then be more collected in your reaction to community living.

Everybody has a level of awareness within them, even when they are not sitting in meditation. In Thailand when the farmer tills the land he is thinking and has to have a certain level of awareness, otherwise he would not be able to complete his tasks. But 'collected awareness' will come only through continued, sustained meditation practice.

## Just Voices

At the beginning the mind is restless. As soon as I started sitting my mind would suggest: 'Maybe you should walk.' So I started to walk. Then the mind suggested I should stand. So I stood and then the mind would suggest I should lie down. Or at other times the deluded mind would suggest that I had no hope of becoming enlightened, so why was I trying anyway? Or it would say: 'You are 16 years old. Why should you not have fun? It is older people who sit still in meditation with eyes

closed, hours on end. Why not have fun while you are young?'
Or the deluded mind would say: 'If you stay a nun all your life,
who is going to look after you in your old age? You had better
get married and have children to take care of you when you are
old.'

It was clear to me that these suggestions were not to be
believed. There was always a place of refuge where I could see
through all these voices which came to haunt me. I understood
the key was to keep on practising, sustain my efforts and
patiently endure.

Finally, walking one night, I felt very still and clear. I had the
firm intuition that I had only to keep going to reap the fruits of
the practice. A small voice inside me said: 'Just keep going and
the beauty of this path will be revealed to you.' So although
there was a mad voice, there was also a sane voice which
encouraged and helped me to continue.

## Lightheartedness

First we contemplate the body within the body, the sensations.
What is it like to be in a body? Secondly we contemplate the
feelings as feelings. Thirdly we contemplate the mind. These
contemplations will help us to develop intuitive awareness and
make us see through our desires and deluded mind states. It is
easy to talk, but we must practise to gain insight into what it
means to do it ourselves.

These exercises gave me lightheartedness, a sense of joy, a
sense of appreciating being. It has been very nourishing and I
discovered the true beauty of this human existence. The goal is
to see the ending of our deluded mind state, to attain pure mind
and see the end of suffering.

The reward for this practice is a happy sense of well-being,
gladness, ease, peacefulness within our hearts. We must
patiently endure unpleasant states, whatever we carry, whatever

we have to work with, knowing there will be an ending. This well-being also brings love and compassion for other people.

## Sharpen Your Awareness Like a Sword

To attain higher insight into the ultimate nature of all things is the most rewarding thing you can aspire to. Keep practising whatever happens and sustain a level of mindfulness throughout all activities. If you understand how to practise, if you know what you have to practise with, the practice is timeless. You can keep going any time, any place. It is not important to be in a retreat situation to develop awareness, but you need to have trust in what you do.

When you have a baby who does not grow fast enough, you do not throw it away, you feed it, take care of it, do everything to help its growth. It is the same with practice. You have to water, persevere, cultivate continuously, then the baby will grow as big as its parents and even bigger. You have to keep practising in order to sharpen your awareness like you would a sword. You need concentration to investigate.

If you practise daily, continuously, you see the suffering, the unsatisfactoriness of human life. This keeps me practising. Ignorance is the key. Realizing I am still ignorant, I can see there is still a lot of *dukkha*. Daily life shows me there is suffering in the human form and it is like a cycle. We should not identify with *dukkha*, however, because there is no self to experience the *dukkha*.

Awareness of the impermanent nature of all things, that alone brings me a lot of peacefulness. Seeing impermanence externally, internally and bodily brings us a sense of peacefulness and contentment, but even that is impermanent. As contentment is impermanent, we must keep going.

Practice does not end; it is continuous. If you continue to practise you will have a continuous state of mindfulness, awareness and clear understanding.

We all have defilements and we have our own karma we bring into each life. We are also grasped by desire, trying to hold an identity and to own things. I still feel that I have *klesas* [defilements]. I can practise and rest peacefully in this awareness, but I cannot stand still and not practise. It is necessary to continue to practise, not just for me, but also for everybody.

We cannot just practise until we see a little insight into the nature of things, think, 'This is it' and stop. To practise for a little while, understanding the continuation of emotions, the moods that propel and direct us, and then stop is not beneficial. We still have defilements and clinging to self until we see the end of all defilements. That is when we can stop; it is the finest enlightenment.

## There Is No Nobody Here

If you keep penetrating the conditioned world, seeing the impermanence of it, then you come to a state of emptiness, of realization that there is nobody here right now. We reach between conventional reality and the unconditional world to ultimate truth. We begin to taste what that means. When the sense of no-self comes then there is a sense of universal belonging.

Keep penetrating and investigating into the identification of name and form in the conventional world – the identification of East and West, North and South, Asian and European, thinking, 'This is my body, my house, my town, my country.' If we understand by looking deeply that these are just conventions, we come to emptiness. There is no one out there. Also there is no one here within the body, the feelings, the perceptions, the volition-mind formation or the consciousness either. We go even deeper into that sense of emptiness.

## The Knower Is the Pointer

Your defilements do not have to be completely burnt out before you can see and experience the no-self, because we need to use our defilements to transcend them. We need to know desire, to inhabit desire in order to transcend desire. We need to know clinging to the sense of 'I am' to actually transcend it. Like crossing the sea with a raft, when we reach the other side, we discard it, we do not have to use it anymore.

We keep practising to see the impermanent nature in all things. There is an awareness which we use as a pointer and it stays perfectly still through all this investigation. From self to no-self, it is like travelling, so when there is no more defilement, that is it, we reach awareness, the sense of the watcher, and the knower being the pointer.

There is a lot of travelling to reach the light. It is like something very dirty which we are cleaning until it gleams. By cleaning it, we develop insight, a tool of wisdom. It is not that we ever look at things as *anicca, dukkha, anatta*, repeatedly like that. It is not like a factory processing, but more like there is wisdom, there is insight, so we know it is going to be beautiful. So we keep polishing it. We keep practising to get rid of defilements with clear comprehension and awareness. It is like weeding – we keep uprooting the *klesas* because we keep putting effort in the practice; we keep digging until there is no seed there to grow again.

## Take It Easy

'Nothing, no dharma, no teaching, is worth being identified with.' Ultimate reality cannot be tied to a state. Do not be hasty in this practice, do not take it all too seriously. Do not burden yourself with the practice. You only need to take one step at a time, however long it takes. Respect yourself. By hurrying, wanting to succeed, you do not respect yourself, you do not give yourself a chance. Take it easy. Everyone will get there.

Don't allow yourself to become a defeatist by thinking: 'I do not have enough mindfulness, I shall never get there. I have not cultivated enough good qualities to get there.' Do not allow the self to get in the way of practice by listening to the negative qualities. This again implies no self-respect. Just keep going, giving yourself energy by cultivating the five factors: inspiration, effort, mindfulness, awareness and wisdom; they can take you to the goal of your practice.

We become easily burdened by things we cannot see. Things we can see, we can let go of by seeing through them when they are too much to carry. Identification with self is heavy and the ego sense of wanting to achieve something can make practice overburdening. The heaviness of practice will make us react to it with the sense of self. It is the paradox of wanting to practise to see no-self and yet what is stopping you is you taking that sense of self so seriously.

## Stop Thinking

Stop thinking. There is so much identification with thinking. Thinking can actually stop you practising. When the mind is troubled by thoughts, busy with itself, with clear comprehension and awareness see this just as it is. Do not keep digging, trying to understand thoughts. Just let go. Each time a thought comes up, just let the knower know: 'This is just a thought.' You do not have to go into the thought and make it something you have to understand; trying to make sense of it makes it heavier.

In this practice you cultivate letting go, letting go in your heart and mind. Put your heart and mind above the moods, feelings and emotions that come into your awareness, so you are not crushed by them. Do not react to them; allow your mood, emotions and feelings to be, without creating more causes and effects with them. Just let them dissolve. When a strong emotion arises, do not put yourself right into it by reacting to it, simply allow it to be a temporary guest within your mind, thus allowing it to cease being.

## Being a Nun

In my own practice I sit for an hour, walk for an hour, stand for an hour and lie down for an hour. Being a nun helps me in my practice because I can make a continuous effort. Even though sometimes I might have a dull mind state and cannot see through the rising and ceasing of an emotional state, I can always take refuge in the triple gems. My faith in this life gives me the strength to keep going and helps me to see through the veil of defilements.

It is important for a practising nun to work with the rules she has been given. The maechees [eight precepts nuns] in Thailand are taught to respect the monks because the monks keep many more precepts than the maechees. We respect them because we are trying to help them keep the *vinaya* [monastic code of behaviour] and because we want to give them a chance to be able to practise. We act as a support, a bit like a prop to the monks. It has nothing to do with status. I do not see inferiority or superiority. I see that the form, the *vinaya*, is the basis.

In Thailand Tan Ajahn Dhammadaro, our abbot, is a unique man. He is very fair and liberal, quite a feminist really. There are other monks who actually repel women who want to ordain as maechees. If a maechee comes to a monastery they will tell her to go away; they do not want to have anything to do with the maechees.

All of us monks and nuns have different demands and ways of doing things. We do not live together as a community, we live separate lives, but sometimes they are interwoven with each other. As long as we respect the duties that each of us has, it is all that is needed. It is very clear we do not need to have status and make comparisons. There is no point in judging by equality because we are very different from each other.

## The World of Convention

There is no point in discussing the inequality between the sexes because the point of the practice is to realize enlightenment. We have to learn to work with the tools we have. The nuns have from eight to ten precepts and the Sakyan rules, and that is enough. As long as we are determined to be enlightened we do not need to ask for any more than that. All we have to do is to keep on practising. We do not advance in the practice by eternally comparing ourselves to other people. Our practice is to look internally at greed, passion and delusion.

As we ordain with the aim of reaching and understanding the ultimate truth, conventional reality is not something we attach ourselves to. We see ultimately that a person is neither a man nor a woman. When we have to deal with the world of conventions, we receive it as such and try not to attach ourselves to it. The practice frees us all the time.

If we take up a role, we get stuck in the world of convention and might end up spending most of our time talking about inequality and status. We really have to look at ourselves and examine the reasons for taking that role. We have to persevere with whatever situation we are in to realize how things really are with the ultimate truth. We have to look upon all obstacles as things to work with. Realizing that there is a problem if we get stuck in the problem, we cannot step forward and move from where we are in order to grow. This stops the progression on the path.

There is a path here – let's hold hands and walk together on this path in harmony and friendship! The goal is transcendence. In the end our bodies will be cremated, and the flames of a woman's body and a man's body do not burn with a different colour. We all go in the same way.

If you believe there is a self, if you believe in conventional reality, how can you reach transcendence?

## The Dharma Is Timeless

Ultimate truth and conventional reality exist together. We try to see and understand both realities. It does not mean we practise until we reach emptiness and then attain the state of ultimate truth. But we all have the possibility of touching that reality, tasting that ultimate truth, as long as we have awareness, concentration and wisdom.

The dharma is not bound up in time, it is timeless. Therefore anyone who wants to take up practice can do so. It does not depend whether you are lay or monastic, male or female. If you have found a method of practice, now you know the way and have the map to get there, so just do it. Because I wear certain robes does not mean that automatically I shall achieve wisdom. All of us have to walk the same path to get there. Regardless of gender, status, etc., we can all practise. Ultimate truth lies within us.

# 6
# walking on lotus flowers
## I Tsao Fashih

Venerable I Tsao is a young Taiwanese nun, one of the foremost
practitioners in the Pure Land tradition at Fo Kuang Shan
temple in Taiwan. I found her lively and happy, and she left me
with a wonderful feeling of joy. Her eyes sparkled, her smile
was warm and her singing voice inspired me to believe in the
Pure Land.

Shakyamuni Buddha himself said there is a Pure Land where Amitabha Buddha resides, so we believe this. Amitabha Buddha has told us his land is extremely beautiful. If you want to do Pure Land practice, you should first understand it, only then can you practise it. How much you understand will determine the depth of your realization. You must understand why Amitabha Buddha wanted to talk about the *Amitabha Sutra*, only then can you have the faith to practise it. You have to know why you want to go to the Pure Land. What is your feeling about going there? Do you have confidence and great faith?

You must practise in your heart. After you believe in the Pure Land outside yourself you will believe there is the Pure Land in your heart. Finally you will see the whole world as the Pure Land.

You know there is America, but you have never been there; you know one day you will go there. It is the same with the Pure Land.

If you aim to go to the Pure Land, then at this present moment you must believe there is a Pure Land. In this way you have confidence and can practise. If someone attains enlightenment, that person can come and go to the Pure Land at will. I am not enlightened, but in my dreams I have been there often.

The responsibility is ours. It is because we commit wrong deeds that we are born into this suffering world; we are here to work out our past misdeeds. Then one day we can go back to the Pure Land.

There are three things to cultivate in Pure Land practice. First there is faith, to believe there is the land of Amitabha Buddha. Secondly you make a vow to go there and thirdly you practise.

For example, first you believe that Fo Kuang Shan temple is in the south of Taiwan. Then you have to make a vow to come here. You can come by aeroplane, bus or car, and you need money to buy a ticket and everything else.

## Golden Trees and Crystal Ponds

Do you want to know the situation of the Pure Land? I know you are more interested in how to practise the tradition, but if you want to know the ways of practising it, first you must know the situation there. Only then can you have the faith, the interest and the confidence to practise. If not, you might give up half-way.

The land is full of golden trees and the ponds are as beautiful as crystal. Here you are not worried about traffic, or aeroplanes crashing. There are lotuses; the smaller lotuses are as big as Taiwan. It is very comfortable here and you can sit on a lotus flower at will. You can travel just as you wish, freely, you do not need a passport. If you like to wear beautiful clothes, you will be wearing them naturally. If you want to eat good food, it will appear at once in front of you. Whenever you think, you get what you want.

The Pure Land is called the highest happiness. I am the happiest and the richest person in the world. Every day in the office I listen to the chanting and my mind is filled with the Pure Land when I am working. When I walk I am stepping on lotus flowers, so I am always happy. When I pass away I will go to the Pure Land; however, I realize that right now too I am living in the Pure Land.

## Let It Be

I am trying to live in a peaceful way. Whenever someone tries to argue about something, I say to myself, 'Let it go, let it be.'

Slowly I try to get rid of all the problems so that I live in a peaceful way every day. In my daily life I try to say only good things about people.

One day I dreamed that I went to the Pure Land. There are seven treasures there and someone brought me to see them. I picked up one treasure and exclaimed: 'It is so beautiful!' When I turned around I saw Amitabha. I also saw the treasure tree of Amitabha.

Another time I dreamed I saw trees which grew diamonds and I wondered why diamonds would grow on trees. I saw a small girl in Amitabha's land and asked her if I could bring back one of the trees. I picked up a tree which was a foot (0.3m) long. At the end of the tree there was a lotus and this lotus I present to you.

Three years ago I went to a museum and there were many precious stones. The guide wondered if I wanted to see them more closely. I told him it was not necessary because all the real precious stones are in the Pure Land. I mean the treasure is in my heart, so I do not need artificial diamonds.

What it says in the *Amitabha Sutra* is real. It is not something you have to believe, it is real, the Pure Land is real. There is a boat to go to the Pure Land and I have also dreamed of this. My dreams increase my faith in the Pure Land. Would you like to go to the Pure Land?

For 10 years I sculpted Buddhist statues of Ksitigarbha, Kuanyin, Samantabhadra and Manjusri Bodhisattvas in clay. After these I sculpted Amitabha. I sculpted this Amitabha Buddha to bow and pay respect to, in order to make merit to go the Pure Land. In a dream I saw the statue of Amitabha slowly change into rice and this made me realize that rice helps us keep our bodies healthy.

## The Practice

In my practice I feel Amitabha is helping me. After sculpting Amitabha Buddha, I did another Kuanyin, and two *Mahasattvas* who are protecting the Pure Land. When I finished sculpting these three statues I started to pay respect to the sutra. I read how to practise in the Amitabha school, how to meditate and how to think about Amitabha's Pure Land.

When I discovered the *Amitabha Sutra*, I began to chant it every day 15 times. My dreams are in accordance with the contents of the sutra. In the Pure Land there are six or seven stages and I will continue practising till I reach the highest. I recite Amitabha's name whenever I am working and am not too busy. When I go back to my room after 5 p.m., I recite the sutra again.

When you are familiar with the sutra you can recite it in five minutes. On the way between my room and the office I recite it three times. I also chant Amitabha's mantra. After 30,000 repetitions you know that Amitabha is in your head, but it is not done in a day. The sutra teaches me to reflect on the greatness of Amitabha.

Sometimes I do a special practice where for one week I chant Amitabha's name. Many people gather, walk and chant his name. When I return to my seat, I see that Amitabha is so great and big I can only see his body, I cannot see his head.

In my dreams I see the statues of Amitabha and Kuanyin and I pay respect to them. They are standing under trees on an altar which is very beautiful. Amitabha is holding my hand and sitting on a lotus, like a mother holding a child.

Each day I pay respect to the Buddha many times. In my room there is a small altar with sculptures of the Bodhisattvas which I bow to more than 100 times every day.

By chanting the Buddha's name and chanting the sutra I will acquire much merit. All the merits I acquire I shall transfer to other people and then I shall be able to go to the Pure Land.

## I Am the Richest Person

When I have time I practise and I also help the monastery by working in the office. I have been a nun for more than 10 years; before, I was an accountant in an office in Taipei. I wanted to learn about Buddhism, to become a nun and practise, but I could not find a suitable place. I dreamed of a mountain and had the feeling the Buddha was there. That place was like a lotus land, but there are many mountains in Taiwan and I did not know where to look or go.

First I went to the Yungmin nunnery where Venerable Hiu Wan used to teach, but I was too old to join the course of study. I was 31 and the course was only for those up to 30. Then I heard of Fo Kuang Shan and that nuns could enter the course of study up to the age of 35. So I went and joined.

One day I was doing some chanting to Kuanyin, and at the end of it I walked and looked up at the mountains. I realized that they were familiar and that I had dreamed of these very mountains. I went back to bow in the Kuanyin Hall because I understood that I had found the place I had been looking for.

For the course of study I had to learn Buddhist art. I was not very interested in it because I did not think I could do art, but my teacher was very inspiring. I asked her how to draw and sculpt a lotus, and from this I started to have an interest in sculpting. After I carved the lotus I decided to sculpt Buddhist statues.

I am the accountant so I have to count bills, but I have no problem with this because as I count each bill I recite the name of the Buddha Amitabha, Amitabha! In my mind and heart, it is all Amitabha. I am very happy, I am the richest person. Everywhere in my house, in my mind is Amitabha. The trees outside, inside me, everything is the Pure Land.

You have to have faith and practise, and then I shall meet you in the Pure Land. Anyone who practises Buddhism and meditates can go there. Meditation is not separate from chanting. The practices of Pure Land and Zen are not different, and you can do both at the same time. Zen is not apart from Pure Land and Pure Land is not apart from Zen. So you too can go to the Pure Land and we can meet there.

# 2

# Training the Mind

# the water and the wave
## Myongsong Sunim

Unmunsa is a large Korean seminary for 300 Buddhist nuns.
Its success is due to the abbess and main lecturer Myongsong
Sunim, one of the foremost sutra lecturers in Korea and widely
respected. Unmunsa goes from strength to strength, has more
facilities, contented students and an atmosphere of peace and
harmony. Myongsong is about 60 but looks much younger.
She is lively and calm, stern and friendly in equal measure,
and always concerned about the welfare of her student nuns.
Some nuns feel the abbess deals with them well because she
cares for plants. Patience is necessary to grow orchids and
trees, and each requires a different way of being looked after.
In the same way, the abbess seems to know how best to deal
with different students.

## What Is the Teaching of the Buddha?

We must know the real meaning of the Buddha before we meditate or pray. If we practise blindly it is possible to miss the target completely. We need to inquire into the teaching of the Buddha before we can present incense or bow to the Buddha. We must know the sutras to be able to chant to the Buddha. This is why I studied the sutras.

First you must produce the right mind when studying the sutras. When the Buddha practised at the beginning there was a reason for his practising. Why did he do so? In the same way, going to the market to buy something definite is totally different from going to the market just because a friend is going or without any aim.

Ever since I was very small I have read a lot of religious books: Buddhist, Confucianist, Christian, even Socrates. I wanted to become such a great sage. Mostly I read Buddhist books and wanted to walk that path. When I saw other people I wondered about the meaning of their lives, as they seemed to be living such empty lives. I decided to become a nun when I was 23.

## The Beginning Mind

When we start we must enquire: what is our motivation? What is it that we are striving towards? We need a fundamental intention, so we start by studying the *Chobalshim* text [*The Beginning Mind*]. The mind is very important. What is the mind we should generate? What is the mind like? The thing that is the mind has no form, no colour. This substance we cannot see with the eyes nor hear with the ears; what is it?

It is essential to continue uninterruptedly with the motivation we started with. The beginning mind, middle mind and finishing mind must all be alike. If the mind generated at the beginning changes, you might do unwholesome or inappropriate actions.

The beginning mind must be continued into the following mind; they are one. In the *Chobalshim* it is said: 'With the first mind of generation one will obtain the right enlightenment.' I often talk about the one mind and how it must not become two.

## The Water and the Wave

If you have erroneous views you might think meditation and study are opposed. It is absolutely not so. If the Buddha's mind is meditation, the Buddha's words are his teachings. The Buddha's teachings do not exist outside the Buddha's mind.

It is the same as the water and the wave not being different. If moving water is a wave, when it quietens down it is still water. The wave that moves and the water that is quiet are not two different things. In the same way meditation and the teaching are not different.

In everyday life there is nothing which is not meditation. When we face the wall and sit, enquiring, 'What is the mind?', everything in our lives becomes meditation. From when we wake up in the morning to the time we lie down at night, we enquire: 'What is it that is lying here?' If we quietly think about it, lying here could be compared to being a living corpse. This is a form of study.

The Buddha's teaching is only an expression of the Buddha's mind using words as communication. Some people do not know that they are one and not two. A meditator might say study is superficial and a student might slander meditators, saying they are ignorant, but these are mistaken views.

## Daily Life

Whether we bow to the Buddha or weed the ground, we must do it with exactly the same mind. If we bow to the Buddha because he is sitting high up, this is idol worship. If we bow to the Buddha while we think the Buddha lives outside ourselves, this is idol worship. If we think our mind right here is the Buddha, we are bowing to our true nature with respect, we are trying to curb thinking which would lead to self-importance or arrogance. This is the meaning of bowing.

In our everyday lives, during the smallest or the largest task, if we live sincerely, checking everything we do, this directly is the meaning of the Buddha. When we weed the ground, or sweep, or do any kind of work, or pay respect to an elderly person, if we do these actions sincerely and truthfully, this is meditation.

If we have done a lot of meditation but then become angry or greedy, it is worse than never having done any at all. The aim of meditation is to correct angry thoughts, foolish thinking or greedy intentions. We meditate to return to our true, pure minds. If we live a disparate, unwholesome life, it is neither meditation nor study.

I prefer to talk about the dharma in an easy relaxed manner. I try to teach laypeople about living correctly in everyday life. As the lotus flower which grows from dirty mud has a beautiful pure bloom, in the same way laypeople living in the world can flower like the lotus. If they cultivate a good way of living together they are fulfilling the intention of the Buddha.

## Like Water Coming from a Source

Even before we teach someone something we are already humbled. If we tell someone to make merit, we are humbled even by saying this. We must first reflect on our own making of merit.

Before I tell someone not to become angry, I have to watch out to see if I, myself, am able to be patient and not become angry.

When we want to tell somebody something, we should not be loud about it. First we should reflect on ourselves; only then will we have the confidence to teach someone else. We must always do things confidently. But it is hard to be confident, isn't it? It is easier to check other people's actions than our own.

Inspiration must come from ourselves. If we hope to get inspiration from outside, as if it were falling from the sky, this is wrong. Strength must come from ourselves, from our own self-confidence. It should be like water coming out of a source. From where else could we receive it?

Personally, my inspiration did not do anything. All the work that has been accomplished here does not come from me, it comes from all the energy gathered together from several people. It was not accomplished by my strength alone. Because many nuns decided to do this together, Unmunsa became what it is. It did not become successful because I have any extraordinary strength. Any achievement came out of the strength of each nun who is studying here; put together, it crystallized.

When you play tug-o'-war, a group of people is pulling the rope, and because they are pulling it together, it moves. The person in front, or any person, cannot say, 'I am the one who made it move.' It is not one person, it is everyone together who accomplishes something.

One cannot convey one's meaning to another person. Someone might ask me: 'Why do you live in the middle of the mountain?' I would use a Zen master's answer to reply to this question. 'At the top of the mountain, the clouds are coming and going.' This is in sympathy with my heart. One's happiness, one's joy, cannot be explained. If I drink some water, only I can know if it is cold or hot and how hot or cold. For this reason I cannot convey the feeling I experience in being a nun.

## The Original Idea of the Precepts

Nuns and monks pay much more attention and put more emphasis on morality than people in secular life. If we look at the rules closely, for the bhikkhu there are 250 precepts, for the bhikkhuni there are 338, for laypeople there are five or 10 and for the sramanera there are 10.

I have discoursed on the bhikkhuni precepts many times. Personally, looking at the original precepts, I feel it is not necessary to follow them extremely closely. The original idea of the precepts is 'to forsake evil and practise good'. This is enough. If we only hold the original idea of the precepts, it becomes second nature; we automatically keep the precepts without having to be told: 'Do this, don't do that!' Do not commit evil and take as your foundation the making of good actions! This is ultimately the teaching of the Buddha.

## Concentration and Wisdom

Our minds are like the waves on the sea, swaying all the time. Concentration helps this swaying mind become still, to find in the midst of our minds the thought which has no dizziness. It is said: 'Do not grasp at outer circumstances, what you can see, what you can hear. Let it rest at once.'

The state in which my inner mind is not grasping, not excited, not busy, is a state where my mind has settled down completely, in the same way as the water settles down. The sea of the mind, the deep water of the mind, when it settles quietly, this is concentration.

However busy you might be, you must have more composure, be cautious and more attentive. In the settling down you ask yourself: 'How could I solve this?' If you have the right concentration, however difficult, however busy your work might be, you are not hard-pressed or strained, you are even more composed. If you have the right concentration power, the right kind of strength will be produced to deal with any circumstances. The pupil of the eyes of a meditator are fixed, they are not going all over the place. This is because of concentration.

If the water of the mind settles quietly, the mind becomes clearer and shines behind all reflections. Due to concentration, wisdom naturally emerges and is evident. The wisdom of the Buddha is not obtained in the same way we would obtain material things. When the mind settles down, at once the light of wisdom shines forth.

Master Bojo said: 'To have no wrongdoings in the midst of the mind is the precepts, to have no giddiness in the midst of the mind is concentration, to have no foolishness in the midst of the mind is wisdom.'

## The Two Wings of a Bird

There is no difference between the monks and the nuns. They are both disciples of the Buddha. They are like the two wings of a bird. Our mission in life is to spread the Buddha's teaching.

## Unmunsa

In Unmunsa there are several departments. There is the department of education whose aim is to spread the dharma. There is the department of culture which produces a newsletter. There is the department of social activities which organizes bazaars, whose income is sent to leper colonies, old people's homes and orphanages. Our nuns visit places where people are suffering as an embodiment of the Buddha's compassion.

Our task is to teach the meaning of the Buddha. These are the guidelines of the college: we must produce a powerful wish by cultivating our intention. We must be diligent and devote ourselves to everything we do without ever being lax. We must not revert to our old behaviour patterns and must always have the same diligence. We must circulate the Buddhist teachings because the Buddha said the wheel of the dharma must turn continuously.

When I first came here there were about 70 nuns. In 22 years many things have happened and the number of nuns has greatly increased. Now there are about 230 students. If we add up everybody who works here in some capacity, we are 257 in all. In the future I expect wonderful nuns with a greater intellect than I will appear and develop this temple even more.

I tell all the nuns that they must become awakened beings. By their own accomplishments they must become good knowing advisors. They must not kowtow anywhere they go. We must all become great women of the Way.


## Living in Harmony

To start with I was not keen on becoming an abbess. My intention was to research and teach the sutras in the capital. However, the nuns of Unmunsa decided that I was to be their lecturer and later asked me to become the abbess. What I like about being an abbess is that I have a free hand to make the students as comfortable as possible. If I were only a lecturer I would have to ask the abbess for desks, curtains, photocopier, etc. and this could be restrictive. Since I am the abbess I can supply whatever the nuns need.

Living in harmony is the aim of this sangha. When nuns find they have different ideas, they should try to understand the others' point of view. If I look in a mirror I see my face reflected in it; the reflection is neither better nor worse than my face, it is just reflected as it is. We must not bear grudges towards other people. All errors must be re-examined in light of ourselves, and together we must be patient and humble.

We advocate living with humility. In this way although 250

nuns are living together, fights or arguments do not happen very often. Anyway, they have to study diligently, clean the grounds, and plant flowers and vegetables, so they are too busy to have time for contention.

## Great Love and Great Sadness

The word for compassion in Korean is beautifully composed of *ja*, which is 'love', and *bi*, which is 'to commiserate, to be sad'. This word, 'compassion', is also compounded with the word 'great'. We always talk of great compassion.

In secular life people love partially. They think, 'I hope everything goes well for my son or my daughter.' They do this when they pray also. To such compassion you cannot add the prefix great.

Great sadness means that when someone falls into a lot of suffering, we spend much energy to get them out of it. It also means that when sentient beings are sad, we are sad with them. When they cry, we also cry. Great love means that when sentient beings are happy, we are happy with them. Being sad together, being happy together, this is great compassion. Great love means that we give great happiness; great sadness means that we deliver people of their suffering.

The idea of compassion is beautiful. Gandhi said he learned the love of mankind from Christianity, but from Buddhism he learned the love of all sentient beings. Everything is included, even a mosquito. This is an impressive idea, to love all sentient beings equally. Therefore, so as not to have anything killed, we do not eat meat. If I care for my life, I also become caring for other life forms and cannot kill any being. Then compassion can flow.

# 8
## enlightened education
## Hiuwan Fashih

Hiuwan Fashih is a Chinese nun of the Tientai school, living in Taiwan. She is 81, and a painter, meditation master, scholar and educationalist. Recently she built a technological college which now holds 600 students. Despite her age she is incredibly active and lively; strict and kind at the same time.

## The Buddha Has to Come Down from the Mountains

I have been interested in education and Buddhism for a long time. In 1942, during the Japanese war, I was staying in a temple on Mount Omei in China. One morning, reading the poetry of an ancient monk, I had my first thoughts about becoming a nun to get away from the entanglements of the world. I started to live in a temple and teach at a nuns' school. Later I visited India for a while. When I came back, I founded four schools in Hong Kong and taught Chinese refugee children.

I was asked to paint a Buddha, so I read many books on Buddhist art. I spent six years doing 10 paintings. Till then I had liked Chinese culture and art and the Confucian classics, but my mind had not been open. After I did these 10 paintings, I realized life was like a painting. Previously I had no strong feeling for the Buddha, nor was I touched by anything around me; I liked ideas. But by painting these Buddha pictures something was released.

Some of the pupils I taught were poor and dirty. I asked the Buddha: 'I am alive and of life, they are also alive and of life. Why are they so poor?' This was the Buddha, the kindness inside. I realized the artist is full of compassion because she looks and has to be aware in order to paint. Buddha's compassion and wisdom – even after 40 years these words trigger a response within me. I became a nun not only for myself, but because Buddha has to come down from the mountains to the ordinary people who are suffering.


## Education Is Not Only Academic Learning

I am concerned about the decline of ethical values in this technological age, and think the humanities should be incorporated into the curriculum of science and technology studies.

Education should not stop at imparting academic learning, but should also teach ethical values. For this reason I embarked on founding the Huafan Institute of Technology in 1987.

For a long time I had wanted to create a college for Chinese culture and Buddhism in Taiwan, but the Ministry of Education does not allow colleges of humanities anymore. They want colleges where the students learn practical skills so they can find work. I realized that architecture is also an art, so we decided that our college would be dedicated to architecture and the technology surrounding its study.

We have a Buddhist club, but not Buddhism as a subject. However, since I am a Buddhist nun and the founder, this has a certain influence on the way the college is run, and the students invite me to teach meditation. I hope they will be inspired by Buddhist values and learn an appreciation of art.

Enlightened education purifies the mind. It does not come from language or books – when you look at something and have a good feeling inside, that is when you have learned something. If the students reflect more on life, they will be able to understand it more. The practice of morality, understanding the perfection of wisdom and having compassion for others are the principles of this technological college.

## Education for Enlightenment

My master was Venerable Tan Hsu and he dedicated his life to education. When he died, his eyes were open and when I made my vow, then and there, to also dedicate my life to education, his eyes closed.

It is not for me, nothing is for me. What is important is the college and the institute, and research into Buddhist education. Technology and culture must contribute to each other, and I want to do this for society. I hope to have technology, culture, Buddhism and art all together.

Education was originally meant to teach people to 'reach the highest good'. Today education is very developed, but it does not seem to succeed in helping young people reach that highest good. An ideal education not only imparts knowledge, it also includes methods for purifying the mind, for remaining undisturbed by worldly objects and for attaining transcendent wisdom. Education for enlightenment means nurturing illumination and transmuting consciousness into wisdom.

## Natural Education

The best education develops our character and teaches us how to find enjoyment in our own way. Combining a natural environment with education creates numerous possibilities and is successful. India has long seen the necessity for education among natural surroundings in order to achieve spiritual and physical growth.

A small grass root, a grain of sand; each is the universe in miniature, and enables us to perceive the relationship between the individual and the world, and the boundless nature of imagination. Nature and human beings are interdependent and interactive and should live together in harmony. Then a culture free from limitations will come into being spontaneously.

Buddha's 'natural education' is the process of enlightenment; it is man's innate nature to reach towards this enlightenment. 'Natural education' does not only mean teaching knowledge and cultivating love and compassion, but also actual practice and experience.

The environment for education should be away from the noise and dust of urban areas, among the tranquillity of the woods. Living quarters should be simple and pleasant. The learning environment should be decorated with literary and artistic works, and contain objects conducive to religious thoughts and meditation. Academically, the power of imagination and the quality of compassion should be emphasized.

## A Good Remedy

If we want to purify our minds from the worries of worldly affairs and achieve permanent wisdom, we need to become internally enlightened and familiar with quietness and tranquillity. A peaceful and wise mind will help us discriminate good from evil.

Ordinary education emphasizes the imparting and acquisition of information. Enlightened Buddhist education trains in both information and morality, and aims at eradicating delusion and revealing wisdom. The ideal Buddhist education is to achieve the goal of teaching and learning simultaneously.

This age of knowledge explosion and advanced technology seems to be progressing in leaps and bounds. But the more advanced human knowledge becomes, the more lonely and desperate the human mind is. It is time to probe deeply into the exact needs of human beings.

How can young people develop confidence? Purifying their thoughts brings compassion and wisdom, then everything in their environment is seen as valuable and they reach true appreciation of the interdependence of things. In this way young people can contribute to this world, striving and planning for the better development of everything in it.

## Quietness and Liveliness

I meditate in everything I do. When I was younger I investigated a Zen koan for eight years. I fought day and night, but always felt something remained untouched and the doors inside myself seemed to be locked.

Master Tan Hsu taught the *Lotus Flower Sutra* in Hong Kong.

He was of the Tientai school and had come from eastern China. When I found the *Lotus Sutra* and the Tientai school, I had a very clear feeling. The first time I met my teacher it changed my mind and my thoughts. There were so many principles and truths worth learning from the Tientai tradition.

I have been practising samatha [concentration leading to quietness] and vipassana [insight leading to liveliness] since 1953. It is important to understand the state of 'quietness and liveliness'. If we do not, we cannot understand meditation. Our meditative state must be clear and lively.

## The Tientai School

The essential tenets of the Tientai school are based on the *Lotus Sutra*. The three great ideas mentioned in the second chapter on 'expedient devices' of equality, independence and undauntedness are interrelated. These are the radical aims of Tientai.

Equality means no discrimination between Buddhas and sentient beings; everyone has the same Buddha nature. Only from equality of mind can love and compassion arise. Independence indicates the enlightened nature of all humanity which brings forth the brilliance of life. Undauntedness means a person with great love and compassion will not be daunted by anything. If everyone can act from these three radical aims, there will be a world full of human dignity and brightness.

In the Tientai school, the whole Buddhist system of thought is called 'study and meditation'. The study, together with meditation, means the absence of contradiction between intellectual knowledge and spirit. By the mutual effect of practice and intellectual research, which is in accordance with causality, the wonderful dharma is brought forth.

In the Tientai system of samatha/vipassana, both concentration and wisdom are complete. It is said: 'Samatha is the first step in subduing the mental factors which fetter men to suffering, vipassana is the vital means to get thoroughly rid of bewilderment.'

Tientai distinguishes three kinds of stillness – samatha – and insight – vipassana – that is, stilling the mind through ceasing to discriminate between opposites, practising skilful means in accordance with conditions and understanding truth, and the three insights into emptiness, conditioned existence and the middle way. All this is devised in order to adapt the methods to the varying capacities of people.

## Regulating the Mind

When you are already inside the hall, why do you still ask: 'Where is the door?' You might go to this or that place looking for something else, but you have to always come back. When you understand the problem of life and death you will not feel so sleepy in meditation.

In the middle of the night when all is still, if we contemplate the mind in solitude we find there is a pure and limpid clarity at its core. We become directly conscious of a state of luminous self-awareness. Then we know we have attained the state of meditation [dhyana].

The way to calm the mind is to regulate it. Buddhism abounds in methods of regulating the mind, one of which is breath counting. This is to count the breaths from one to ten and apart from counting, no other thoughts should intrude. If you are distracted by other thoughts, then you must start counting from one all over again.

At the beginning you can count 'one' each time you breathe in and out, as your mind will be very untidy. Later, when your mind becomes clearer, you can try to count one, two, three, up to ten. If you think about something else, you will forget to count, so you have always to come back to the counting. This is like kindergarten, but your mind will slowly become calmer till after a while you can count to ten without being distracted. This is samatha.

Following this, you can chant the name of Amitabha Buddha: '*Amitofo, Amitofo.*' You start by saying it loudly, then you say it softly inside. Reciting *Amitofo* can make our thoughts very tidy.

First you have to hold the ox firmly, then you can let the ox free because it is no trouble anymore.

## Resting in Stillness

Most of us do not understand what is meant by 'stillness', even though we sit motionless. We find it hard to rest in stillness because our minds and bodies do not function accordingly; thus though the body is motionless, the mind is running riot with all kind of thoughts. In breath counting, the practitioner is not really in stillness as their mind is still counting. However, this kind of organized exercise trains the distracted mind to be disciplined.

The sequence of practices is first breath counting, second following the course of the breath, third stillness, fourth contemplation, fifth returning, sixth purification. It is a step by step process which requires patience.

There are three stages of meditation training which lead to great wisdom. The first consists in calming the mind. All day thoughts come to trouble us and there is no time for asking deeper questions, but however busy we are we must set aside time to concentrate on the deeper meaning of life.

The second consists in purifying the mind. If we calm the mind and inquire into what life really is, we find the world is impermanent. If we understand the transitory nature of our lives, we will understand their non-existence. If we understand this, then we understand the non-existence of our egos. Then we do not worry overmuch about whether we succeed or fail, gain or lose, possess something or not. This tranquillity saves us a lot of mental disturbance and our mind is not troubled by frustrations or heartened by successes. Instead, it is purified and we experience peace.

The third consists in turning our minds into Buddha-minds. Purifying the mind for our own sake stops short of our Buddhist goal. A true Buddhist cannot simply meditate in a wood. However, you may live temporarily in a wood to work out ways for everyone to reach enlightenment. We must ultimately share the afflictions which trouble all beings and try to relieve them. It is because we understand emptiness that we can shower boundless compassion on all beings unconditionally, as parents do with their children.

## Wisdom and Self-Knowledge

The essential basis for the development of a modern Buddhist culture consists of developing wisdom. Wisdom is like water, for it can cleanse our mind, and is like a mirror in which our minds are clearly reflected. Wisdom can purify us, giving us light and strength. Through the penetration of wisdom we can develop ourselves and share what we have understood with others. This is the spirit of love and compassion, which is the basic meaning of the Buddha's message.

We have to clarify our problems and solve them in order to develop wisdom. When we understand this, we take action. If we do not, then it is not true wisdom. We should keep a constant watch over our minds, checking, for example, whether we are lying or honest. Often we become friends with our delusions without realizing it. We brood on matters of little importance and have negative thoughts about people we have differences with. When we are unhappy, there is mental war within.

How do we know which thoughts are detrimental to our

mental well-being? This requires the practice of contemplation and self-examination. Our minds must be empty for something else to be able to come in. Then we become free to take up or leave our problems.

Self-respect is important. When studying Buddhism, do not think about your weaknesses but about your strengths. You have to respect yourself as well as respecting other people's virtues and being encouraged by them. Self-respect is essential and different from arrogance. Also, if you respect others, they will respect you. We do not look down on anybody else, but respect our own virtues and our own personality because our virtue brings wisdom.

## Walking Slowly

Meditation and ethics cannot be separated. If we are disciples of the Buddha we must keep the precepts, and when sitting we must sit still and straight. If we are nuns, we represent Buddhism, so we must be careful in words, actions and body. When we walk we must not rush, but walk slowly, step by step. When a 90-year-old nun in Hong Kong crossed the road she was so dignified that all the cars stopped. If we follow the precepts the Buddha will protect us.

It is important to know whether you have an ethical attitude or not. If you do something, it is dharma only if it is within an ethical context. Doing things for yourself only, this is not dharma. When you do something, it must not be contrived. The dharma is wonderful. You can do whatever, you can go wherever, but the master will keep an eye on you. If you are doing something wrong, it will not work, because dharma is awareness.

There is a saying about the 'worm that dies inside a book'. It means if you cannot recognize the meaning or principle of the sutras, they will not be beneficial. If you do not practise what you read and just believe the words, you will die like a worm inside a book. You must go into the sutras, but also come out and make use of them. Then you will be using the dharma.

The Buddha's mind is compassion. It is very good for us to have compassion, so you always want more. I believe strongly that the sutras are the dharma, but you must make the Buddha's words come alive now, not 2,500 years ago. The Buddha is alive now; this is Buddha's place.

## The Painting in One's Heart

In my seventh year of learning painting I was in tears, frustrated because I still could not paint as well as my teacher. I thought of giving up painting to learn medicine. Then someone pointed out to me that if I took fright at the sight of blood, how could I take up medicine? So I plodded on with my painting and literature.

My teacher told me to wait another three years. As practice makes perfect, after 10 years of practice, I could work magic with my paint brush. I could paint whatever I wanted. I had laid a solid foundation during those 10 years.

Ordinary painters paint for the sake of painting, but painters who meditate paint after the paintings in their hearts, which appear naturally, cherished as something natural, not primarily for the sake of being painted.

An ancient Chinese poet and calligrapher said: 'At first I did not understand painting, but through practising contemplation of the truth of Buddhism, I became aware of the emergence of spontaneity.' This emergence of spontaneity is what one should struggle for. Art originates from wisdom. Chinese painting is rich in poetic beauty and its theories about painting are also applicable to literature and the principles of life.

Here is a poem – or it may be called a painting:

*My heart is like a brilliant autumn moon,*
*Shining over a clear cool lake.*
*Nothing can be compared with its purity,*
*How can I express this?*

# a gradual path
## Ani Thubten Chodron

Ani Thubten Chodron is an American nun from the Tibetan Gelugpa tradition. She is engaging and passionately devoted to her Buddhist life.

## What Is the Meaning of My Life?

When I was younger I was taught that having a big house, a nice car, lots of family and friends, and a big name made one successful. However, as I matured this no longer made sense and by the time I graduated from college I was disillusioned with the system. Society was so strange during the Vietnam war, I could not reconcile myself to its values. I felt education was the promise, the answer, so I decided to concentrate on children, to educate them in a positive way to create a better society and to this end I became a teacher.

After marrying a young lawyer, I travelled to Europe, North Africa and Asia. I did not know anything about Buddhism at the time, though I saw Buddhist things and found them vaguely interesting. My husband and I brought back many Buddhist artefacts to put on the walls of our flat, not because we believed in Buddhism but because we wanted a lot of exotic things that people would admire when they came to visit.

Back in the USA, I began teaching elementary school in Los Angeles and going to graduate school. In 1975, one day I saw a flyer about a meditation course and although I was not actively searching for anything spiritual at the time, I decided to go. I had everything one was supposed to be happy with: a nice husband, a good job, interesting studies, many friends. Everything was superficially OK, but I felt something was missing, though I did not know what it was.

When the summer vacation came I signed up for this meditation course, which was taught by Lama Yeshe and Lama Zopa. It changed everything. What struck me about the dharma was the emphasis on motivation. It made me start looking at *why* I was doing things instead of *what* I was doing. The dharma identifies anger and attachment as negative mental states which cause suffering to self and others. I had never really thought about how suffering came from my own mind before.

Turning within and looking at my own attitudes and feelings when there was something unpleasant in my life was new. It shook me up, because I had thought I was a pretty nice person till then. Once I started meditating and looking at why I was doing what I was doing, I could only point to a few tiny unselfish acts in my whole life. When I looked honestly, I saw that everything was done from self-interest and was often accompanied by attachment and anger.

Initially the doctrine of rebirth did not completely make sense to me, but the more I thought about it, the more it did. When I put rebirth together with the fact that my mind was basically out of control, I became concerned with what was going to happen in my next rebirth. When I was a child, I used to ponder on death, which always instigated thoughts such as: 'If I die, what is the meaning of my life? What is the meaning of doing anything, if when I die I have to leave everything?' When Buddhist teachers started talking about death, it confirmed my musings and I had to rethink what I was doing with my life and the effects my actions would have on future lives.

## A Gradual Path

The first meditation I did was *Lam Rim*, which in Tibetan means 'the gradual path to enlightenment'. We were taught some breathing meditation, but mainly the *Lam Rim* analytic checking meditation. *Lam Rim* is a gradual path to enlightenment, with step by step instructions about what meditations to do when and in what order. This enables the teachings to be clearly organized in one's mind. It trains the mind in a gradual way to think constructively. I found the analytical meditation very helpful because I am a thinker; the university world was my home. Learning to think in realistic and beneficial ways while meditating fitted very well with my personality.

For example, when we meditate on death, the first step is to reflect that death is inevitable; we think about the fact that everybody is going to die and that there is no place you can go to avoid death. Secondly, we think that the time of death is uncertain; we do not have a fixed lifespan, small things can cause our death and there is no guarantee that we will live long. Thirdly, we ponder on what is worthwhile at the time of death, when we leave behind our body, our friends and relatives, and possessions. Thinking like this causes us to reflect on what is really important in our lives.

This point by point method gave me a way to understand my life. I was not the kind of person who wanted to sit, meditate and learn to concentrate. I wanted to figure out what life was about. The *Lam Rim* teachings gave me a philosophical and psychological framework with which to look at my whole life, to put things in proper perspective so they made sense. What were my good qualities? What was my garbage? *Lam Rim* showed me clearly what to do when my garbage – self-centredness, clinging attachment, anger and so forth – appeared. When anger arises, the *Lam Rim* instructs us to look at the situation in another way; when attachment arises, we apply another perspective. There are many antidotes, many different ways to view our situations, so that our experience of them changes.

Instead of being carried away and acting in a way that hurts other people, when these emotions came up, I could pause and reflect: 'These are negative emotions. How can I look at the situation differently? How can I frame this situation so that my reactions naturally change and negative emotions do not arise?'

It is not a question of ignoring the emotions or suppressing them; it is an attempt to look at the situation in a new way so that anger and jealousy do not emerge. To see certain emotions and thoughts as negative mental states was revolutionary for me. Till then I had seen them as good; I thought that if I did not get angry, people would step on me or take advantage of me.

When we understand what causes a negative mental state, then we can apply one of the many appropriate antidotes. For example, we can put ourselves in the other person's shoes and look at the situation from their point of view. Usually when we are angry and look at a situation, we think we are seeing an objective reality, but in fact we are seeing the situation through the filter of I, me and mine. When we see the situation from the other person's point of view, it looks completely different. When we think how our own actions might appear to the other person, we might understand why this person does not like us or why they are behaving in this way. I find this very useful and apply it to my interactions with others.

Through dharma practice there has been a definite change in my mind. I used to be quite sarcastic, sharp-tongued and critical, and now I am not as emotionally up and down. I do not get depressed and my mind is steadier. My relationships with people have improved, especially since I began to watch my speech. Being aware of body, speech and mind is the practice of mindfulness, of seeing negative attitudes as they arise and correcting them before they cause pain to ourselves or others.


## The Mind Is the Source of Happiness and Suffering

Even though breathing meditation is not stressed in the Tibetan tradition, I find it useful for Westerners. Our minds are very cluttered and breathing meditation helps clear the mind. Watching the breath, we slow down. Then looking at our thought processes without a lot of judgemental words helps us to become friends with ourselves.

Although we usually perceive that our suffering and happiness come from outside, our minds are the source of our happiness and suffering. When we observe our experiences, we can see that our own attitudes play a part, so if we can change our attitude, we can change our experience. In meditation we ask ourselves whether attachment brings happiness or not. What are we attached to? What is the effect of attachment in our lives, is it beneficial or not? We can reflect on anger too: is this constructive or destructive? What makes us angry? Why do we become angry? What would happen if we looked at the situation from a different perspective?

As it is traditionally taught in the Tibetan community, *Lam Rim* can be difficult for people who have no meditative or Buddhist background and Westerners generally do not. It is essential for us to look first at our own minds and emotions. Then we can look at the mind from the perspective of rebirth, see it extending from the past to the present to the future. Our minds are a continuum, constantly changing without beginning or end. After this we can understand karma, rebirth and the four noble truths.

When we have an encompassing picture of what life is about, we can begin the *Lam Rim* meditations on precious human rebirth, death, taking refuge and so on. When we have an understanding of the entire *Lam Rim*, then we can take tantric initiations.

## Daily Practice

Whenever something disturbing happens or when harmful emotions come up, I try to reflect: 'What am I feeling? What buttons are being pushed?' I try to look at what is going on inside me as the day goes on and not to let things stockpile until the evening or from day to day. My basic practice is thought transformation. This consists of meditation – also found in the *Lam Rim* – to develop compassion and wisdom and to transform all circumstances we encounter into the path of enlightenment. I apply these meditations to whatever is going on, to work things out. If I am busy during the day, then I do them in the evening.

Recently I have been doing some mindfulness practice as taught in the Theravada tradition. When things arise in the mind, it helps me to just sit and feel them, to accept whatever my experience is at a particular moment. However, I need the understanding which comes from the analytical meditation in order to just sit and feel the emotion.

I am not the kind of person who could do only mindfulness, because I have to be completely convinced, for example, that anger is negative. I cannot just sit there, watch and observe: anger, anger, anger. I have to understand first that it is really a misinterpretation of reality. Checking meditation enables me to do that, and then I can just sit and feel the energy of whatever is arising. I watch how it feels in the body, what the mental feelings are and how it changes.

In general I use a variety of meditations because we need to develop many aspects of our personalities. I choose which meditation to do according to what is strong in my mind at the time, often relying on thought transformation, but at other times doing mantras and visualization.

It is important for us to practise everyday and not to have a 'yoyo mind'. Some people meditate three hours one day and then not for the next five weeks, or they meditate every other day. Even if we have busy lives, we can make time to meditate at least half an hour every day. It is important to do this even when we are tired or sick or think it is not working, because meditation does have an effect.

When we wake up in the morning, it is helpful to make our first thought: 'Today I am not going to harm others. I am going to try to be of benefit to others. Today I want all my actions to be motivated by the wish to become a Buddha for the benefit of all other beings.' Making this our first thought, even before we get out of bed, changes our whole day. Then we get up, wash, make a cup of tea and sit down to meditate straightaway, before doing anything else. Following this, we get into the day's activities, trying to be aware of what we are saying and doing, thinking and feeling, throughout the day. If we lose our centre, we back off, look at our minds and work things out.

At the end of the day, we sit down and review the day; what went well, how were we able to serve others? What attitudes were good? When we are able to abandon acting negatively or do something kind, however small, let's rejoice. People need to rejoice, especially in the West. One of the greatest impediments on the path is negative self-image and low self-esteem; both men and women have it. It generally manifests as not feeling good about, or liking, ourselves. It is important to first feel happy about what we do and how we are, then we can look at what needs to be improved in our actions of body, speech and mind.

Each year I take some weeks to do a meditation retreat. A retreat provides me with time when I do not have to do anything else. It is like a holiday, because generally I am quite busy during the day attending to other people's needs. But during a retreat, the phone does not ring, there is no correspondence, counselling or teaching to do, I can just put the teachings into practice, be quiet and not have to speak. Long retreats are useful when we are ready for them, but if we are not adequately prepared, we can waste a lot of time.

When doing a retreat on a particular deity, a particular manifestation of the Buddha, I do four sessions every day. In the past I did this with a mantra commitment and counted many mantras. I now meditate more and don't emphasize counting mantras. My preference is to spend the time in retreat meditating slowly, experiencing the visualization and the effect it has on me. These practices are not just rituals, they really change the mind.

## The Wisdom Mind

I have made promises to my teachers to do certain meditations daily and these form my basic daily practice. Many days I don't do them very well, but I still feel revitalized and this energy every day is very helpful. If I stay in touch with the energy of Tara, Chenrezig or Yamantaka, for example, then during the day as things arise I respond adequately. By keeping the commitments every day, even if I do not do them very well, that energy is there; I can draw from it and tap into it when it is needed.

When we take an initiation into the practice of a particular Buddha, our teacher asks us to meditate on this Buddha daily. We start by taking refuge and generating an altruistic intention. Then we visualize the Buddha – the omniscient mind in the aspect of a particular deity – and do practices to purify the mind and build up positive potential. It is important to remember the Buddha or deity is not inherently existent; it is not an external god. We imagine the deity coming on top of our heads and dissolving into us. As our minds merge with that of the deity, we meditate on the lack of solid, independent identity, both of ourselves and of the deity. Within that space, our wisdom minds manifest in the appearance of the deity.

This meditation transforms our self-image. We stop grasping at an identity which affirms that 'I am Chodron, I am a nun, I am a woman, I am an American, I have this kind of personality, I can do this and I cannot do that, I hate myself because I am so lousy'. Instead of getting stuck in this solid identity we begin to realize that it is an hallucination, a projection of our minds. We dissolve it and try to see our own wisdom minds appear in a pure form. I do not do my practice very well, but it still creates a space where I do not have such a solid personality, where there is a different potential within me.

I do not recommend to people to learn meditation only from

a book. It is too risky; we may make our own thing up and misinterpret it. We need someone to instruct us how to meditate, to explain how it works psychologically and what the purpose is. Otherwise it is very easy for the mind to misconstrue things. For basic practices we do not need initiations. But to do the complete meditation in which we imagine ourselves as the deity – a tantric sadhana – we need the empowerment [initiation] from a qualified teacher.

I would caution people about taking higher initiations too quickly because I have seen too many people rush in, take a high initiation and afterwards become confused and give everything up. Then there is no benefit to them or to the dharma. It is better to practise simply and put our lives in order. When our lives are together we can begin other practices and perhaps do a Chenrezig or a Tara. But to practise the highest yoga tantra, it is best to wait until we have a firm foundation. Otherwise it is similar to building the roof when we haven't yet laid the foundation or constructed the walls.

Many people have wrong conceptions about Vajrayana; they think it is exotica, magic or a quick and easy path to enlightenment. Some think it is sex or psychic powers. Such wrong conceptions arise because people do not have adequate information or read incorrect books. As His Holiness the Dalai Lama says, Vajrayana is built on the basic practices of ethics, simplicity of life, compassion, love for others and wisdom, understanding emptiness. Only when we have developed some practical understanding of these should we enter Vajrayana. However, Vajrayana can be very skilful if one has right understanding.

## Checking One's Teacher

It is important to have a teacher. Personal connection, an example of somebody who really practises and the inspiration from having the teaching from a real live human being cannot be obtained from a book. A teacher helps us to feel there is some support for our practice, that someone is behind us, so when we have doubts, questions or insecurities we have somewhere to turn. Also, a teacher prevents us from 'doing our own trip'. A teacher with whom we have a good relationship can guide us so we do not go off in the wrong directions. At the beginning, it is important to spend time with our teacher, but as we mature, we do not always need to be with them.

His Holiness the Dalai Lama said that we must check a teacher carefully before we take them as our guru. We must be very careful and understand the purpose of having a spiritual mentor. Forming a relationship with a teacher is about developing our responsibility and our wisdom, it is not about abdicating them to somebody else.

Most of my teachers are Gelugpa, but one is Kagyupa. I do not like to identify myself as a Gelugpa, because there is so much sectarianism. I simply call myself a Buddhist or a Tibetan Buddhist. When I was in Singapore I learned about the Theravada tradition and also Chinese Buddhism, and respect them very much. I appreciate other traditions, draw on them and feel comfortable with them, even though my primary orientation is Tibetan and Gelugpa.

## Women

Many statements are attributed to the Buddha about women. At the beginning I believed everything 100 per cent, so for a while I started to lose confidence in myself. Later I realized that the Buddha could not have said these things for the purpose of making women discouraged and disinclined to practise. This would go against the intention of the Buddha, which is for everyone to develop their potential and become enlightened.

I began to see Buddhism in its cultural and historical setting and to draw on Western sociological, anthropological and historical studies. In this way, we can see Buddhist scriptures and institutions as dependent on the society in which they existed, a reflection of the culture.

In terms of sexism and ways of dealing with discrimination, it is important to reflect on our reactions to it. Whenever I was put down as a woman, I used to react with pride and anger. But when our minds are filled with pride and anger we cannot work positively with anybody else. If we become angry and come on like bulldozers, people feel backed into a corner and we cannot communicate well. My philosophy now is to put my own life together, let go of negative attitudes and live in a straightforward way. If I do so, other people will see this. When somebody makes a sexist comment, if it is appropriate and I can be skilful, then I try to have a discussion with that person and deal with this issue in a sensitive way.

## Closer to Buddha

In 1975, when I first started to practise meditation, the dharma deeply touched my heart. I knew that if I stayed in the same situation – marriage, job, graduate school and friends – I would easily continue in my old pattern of ignorance, anger, attachment and self-centredness. I needed a structure and lifestyle that would help me to change and grow. Becoming a nun would give me this space and so I decided to take ordination.

It required a lot of thought, however, because I knew my parents would be against it. If I stayed in my situation, though, my parents and husband would be happy for part of the time, but I would not be able to make them completely happy. Also, if I had a lot of negative karma on my mind-stream at death I would have an unfortunate rebirth and then could not help anybody. I decided to make a definite change in my character because I did not want to continue to be so selfish, egotistical and proud. Although separating was difficult, my husband supported my ordaining. He is also a Buddhist and we enjoy seeing each other from time to time at Buddhist events.

When I initially met Buddhism I did not consider ordination. The idea of being celibate seemed ridiculous and impossible. However, as I started to look at my motivation for having sex, having a career and being with my friends and family, I discovered that they were not very benevolent. My life was organized around my own ego, my wants and needs, cravings and desires. It became evident that if I continued to live with all these attachments I was going to make a mess not only of my future lives, but also of this life and other people's lives too. I needed discipline and to make some firm ethical choices.

Being a nun for these past 18 years has been very beneficial and satisfying. The monastic lifestyle has given me clarity and a positive direction. Recently I was teaching some people how to meditate on death in order to empower ourselves in our lives. 'Think that you are dying. When you look back on your life, what is it you feel good about and what is it you need to clean up before you die?' When I did that meditation, the first thing that came to mind was that I felt very good about being a nun.

Being a nun has clarified many aspects of my life, especially my relationships to people. For example, when I became a nun I realized how many 'trips' there were between men and women. We try to make ourselves appear in a certain way so others will be attracted to us. Becoming a nun cut off a lot of those games. It meant I would not relate to people in that way. As a nun, I can be much more direct, open and simple with people, both men and women.

As deficient as my dharma understanding is, as weak as my meditation practice is, at least I have been able to keep the precepts. Ordination made me closer to the Buddha. I feel that link wherever I am, whatever I am doing. If I were not a nun, my disturbing attitudes would run rampant. The vows remind me of my practice and connect me with the Buddha, dharma and sangha.

# 10
## the doors of liberation
### Haeju Sunim

Haeju Sunim is a professor of Buddhist studies at the Korean
university of Tongguk. She is bright and composed. To my
great delight I discovered she is a proponent of the
Avatamsaka school, which had a major influence upon
Chinese, Korean and Japanese Zen Buddhism, but has largely
died out nowadays. It was inspiring to meet a nun who lives
according to its radical tenets.

## The *Avatamsaka Sutra*

In the *Avatamsaka Sutra*, it is said: 'All things are made by the mind.' I became a nun because I wanted to study the mind, so I was most interested by this sutra. The more I studied the *Avatamsaka Sutra*, the more I realized the place of practice, of cultivation, was nowhere else but where I was at that moment.

It is said in this sutra: 'The way of the Buddha is in the 84,000 doors of liberation.' So you can see there are thousands of liberation doors, thousands of skilful means. Therefore to go somewhere special and take up a koan is not the only way of practice. Whatever the circumstances, whatever one is doing, anywhere can provide a place to attain liberation. I finally realized that. For this reason, I remained in Seoul and taught at university.

I became a nun to solve the question of mind. I wanted to practise to obtain liberation and freedom. I did not think of studying very seriously, as I presumed I would not get liberation from it. For a while I studied at Unmunsa college and several times I thought a lot about finding a place to practise meditation. As I studied the sutras, however, slowly I started to see it would be essential to know them in more depth. When I graduated from Unmunsa, I went to continue my study in Tongguk University.

After completing my course at university, I planned to do true study, to practise somewhere and meditate far away deep in the mountains, in a quiet atmosphere. But there was another level on the course I was following, so I went to post-graduate school. When I did my master's course, I chose the *Avatamsaka Sutra* as my subject.

## Sentient Beings Are Buddhas

When I was researching the philosophy of the *Avatamsaka Sutra* as related to the origin of the Buddha, I found this statement: 'The mind of sentient beings directly is the mind of the Buddha.' Sentient beings are Buddhas.

Because I did not know that originally I was a Buddha, I could not live like a Buddha. So I was acting like a sentient being. But within me there was limitless possibility, similar to a Buddha's. So I studied the idea that sentient beings and the Buddha are not in different bodies.

For my Masters course I had researched the bodhi-mind that is necessary to become a Buddha. But for my PhD it was not the 'mind to become in the future' but the 'mind that we have originally' that I researched.

My view of what practice is has radically changed. Now I practise in this way, right here in this very place. I am endowed with this Buddha-mind originally, I apply it directly and use it to the best of my ability. This is the essence of my practice. It is important to teach this to anyone who is interested.


## Buddha's Activity

My life is quite different from the nuns who live together in a sangha lifestyle. All my life revolves around the university and I have a professor's schedule. I teach most days from 9 a.m. to 5 p.m.; sometimes I give evening lectures. The rest of the time I do preparation or I reflect on my mind. I also practise some awareness meditation. I write essays about the *Avatamsaka Sutra* and compile them into books.

What is important is our attitude of mind. All my work I see as a Buddha's activity. As it is said in the *Avatamsaka Sutra*: 'In this world, there is not one work which cannot be considered as a Buddha's work, especially if it brings happiness to people. In the Buddhadharma, there is not one dharma that can be rejected.'

When I teach at university, it is different from giving a dharma talk to Buddhist laypeople. Buddhism is a religion and a religion is a faith. In a university one pursues knowledge; students do not come to study Buddhism to enter a belief. One starts from a point diametrically opposed to faith. One must question, investigate, be critical.

Because of this different approach there are a few monks and nuns who say they have lost faith by coming to study here. We must let go of this kind of faith. If we believe in something that we have misunderstood, in time we are bound to meet someone who will redress that misunderstanding. If we continue believing a wrong understanding is a right one, this will not be very helpful to us in our life. What we believed or understood previously, we need to question again and again. Then we can gain right faith, the properly understood belief. By questioning anew, we discover the exact meaning and deepen our faith in the process. I am combining learning and faith. In this way learning is a great help in my life.

This mind we are studying is expressed through actions and words. In our everyday life we think, listen, see. Whatever we are doing is practice, because it is using and manifesting the mind. It is not enough to know extensively the teaching of the Buddha, we have to put it into practice and live it. This is the practice of the mind.

## Flower Garland

The *Avatamsaka Sutra* was taught by the Buddha. What did he want to say to us in this sutra? It is a sutra which expresses the awakening of the Buddha. This is shown through the 'Flower Garland' that is Avatamsaka; the flowers are the Bodhisattva's activities.

The awakened world is not an easy world to talk about. It is difficult to demonstrate to people who are not awakened, who do not see it. In order to make it understandable it is displayed through the activities of the Bodhisattvas, who are showing us the path by which we can live as a Buddha.

When the Buddha awakened, he realized interdependence and Buddhists have expressed this in different ways ever since. The Avatamsaka sect said all things and all beings depend on each other and are one. So this is a world without separation.

'There is nothing which is not Vairocana Buddha.' We are part of the world of Vairocana Buddha which is existing right here. Originally we are the manifestation of the body of Vairocana Buddha and for this reason we must live like a Buddha, in all aspects of our lives. From the point of view of the *Avatamsaka*, when we realize completely that we are a Buddha now, then there is no need for further practice. Then we live like a Buddha and our minds are the Buddha's mind.

## We Are All Buddhas

In the Zen tradition, especially in Korea, it is said that awakening, or the Buddha's realm, cannot be expressed in words; as soon as you utter a word about it, you are in the wrong. Only those who have entered the awakened realm can know each other.

But the *Avatamsaka Sutra* shows the awakened realm, the Buddha's realm. It is so beautiful that, through faith, you can enter it. This awakened realm is not far away and unattainable. Right here you are Buddhas, not knowing that you are.

If you put the Buddha on a pedestal far away from you, it becomes impossible to live like a Buddha. Turn this around and awaken; this is the practice. The mind that believes completely you are a Buddha is the faith from the point of view of the *Avatamsaka*. Determine to live like a Buddha because you are one.

The teaching of the Buddha is to realize enlightenment, but the methods to realize it have changed according to the times. At the time of the Buddha and sometime after it was believed that one could not become a Buddha, however diligently one practised. It was said one could only attain the world of the *arhats* [liberated saints] and liberate oneself to that degree. There was supposed to be only one Buddha, Shakyamuni.

This changed when the Mahayana schools developed, of which the Avatamsaka was one. The Mahayana said that if we practised and lived in the same way the Buddha practised in the past, we too could become Buddhas. To raise the mind to become a Buddha is to raise the mind of unsurpassed enlightenment.

The difference between a sentient being and a Bodhisattva is that sentient beings think they can never become a Buddha and live in this way. Bodhisattvas think they can practise in exactly the same way as the Buddha, cultivate the perfections [*paramitas*] and become Buddhas at some point in time, even if they are not Buddhas now. But for a while it was still assumed to take a very long time, like three aeons.

Next came the One Vehicle school which said it was not necessary to spend a long time becoming a Buddha; it was possible to become a Buddha in one lifetime if you practised diligently. For this reason the great teachers said: 'Do not waste this life, do not wait for another life, do not leave some work to do for the next life, awaken in this lifetime.' In this lifetime, having received this body, there is plenty of opportunity and time to awaken. Many people have awakened and realized their Buddha nature.

However, the *Avatamsaka* says: 'Right here you are a Buddha.' There is no need to become, to attain awakening. Uisang Sunim, a great Korean master of the Avatamsaka sect, said: 'From long ago, already one was a Buddha.'

When I dream, while inside the dream I do not know I am

dreaming. We must wake up from the dream to know we have been dreaming. Now I am a Buddha, but if I am not aware of it, because I do not know I am a Buddha, to 'generate the mind' is to become aware that one is a Buddha. In this very place we can live on a path of happiness. We can display all the wisdom and compassion of a Buddha.

Practising from the point of view of the *Avatamsaka* is to reach the place where we originate. To live according to our original form is to play in the realm of awakening. This realm of awakening is not far away, it is on this very Earth where our feet are walking one step at a time.

## The Golden Lion

'In one thing there are all things,' Uisang Sunim said. He added: 'In all things, there is one thing.' I am one, the other people are many. What is the relationship between the one and the many? It is a relationship where they are living within each other.

However, sentient beings are such that they cannot live within each other. A world where everyone is living, combining with each other is a Buddha's world. All dharmas interpenetrate with each other, they are one. For this reason it is said: 'Form is emptiness, emptiness is form', which means all that exists is one.

It is the same as the wave and the water being one. It is also like making a golden lion. The form is a lion, but it is made of gold. With gold you can make various artefacts, rings, necklaces, earrings, etc. They all have different shapes, but they are all made of gold. The gold does not change, is not different. It is the same with the lion.

So all sentient beings are shaped differently, but they all have the same Buddha nature. It is hidden among what is appearing, in the same way as under the shape of the lion is hidden the gold. The shape of the lion and the nature of the gold are one and form a golden lion.

When you perceive the golden lion, you might see only one thing, generally the shape. A wise person is more likely to see the gold than the lion, because the lion is not very important. But most people might say: 'Look at this lion! It is very big. It looks very fearsome.' A young child is likely to exclaim: 'Look at this lion!' and not: 'Look at this lump of gold!'

According to each person, either the lion or the gold will be seen. If someone sees only the lion, the gold will be hidden; if someone sees only the gold, the lion will be hidden. But in reality they exist together. So it is said: 'The sentient being is truly the Buddha.'

## Learn to See Everything

Hearing this, you might start to see only the Buddha and not the sentient being which is hidden. You might then ask yourself: 'What is there to do, why should I chant? I am the Buddha. Come to worship before me. Why should I bow three times to the great monks and nuns? Why should I perform Bodhisattva activities?' What happens is you only see that your nature is originally the Buddha. You do not see at the same moment that you are also a sentient being.

On the other hand, you might say: 'I cannot do anything, do not ask me anything', because you see yourself as only a sentient being. You cannot see the limitless possibilities offered by the Buddha-nature which is originally hidden within yourself. The problem for either group is that they only see one thing. We must learn to see both at the same time.

In everyday life this happens often. Reading the newspapers, we generally know only the side that is presented by the newspaper. We must learn to look behind our perceptions to discover the whole story. We often live in this way, one-sidedly. It is like walking with a plank on one's shoulder and always seeing only half of the picture.

Similarly, we have a tendency to see only the mistakes of others and not our own. When we are in pain, we only see our pain and will say that someone else's illness is nothing compared to ours. When someone talks, we only follow the words and this results in conflicts. We must look behind the words and see the mind and its intentions.

## Indra's Net

In the *Avatamsaka*, it is said that the 3,000 great worlds can fit into one single follicle of the Buddha's hair. Each follicle has the same capacity. All the universe is contained in one single speck of dust; they are one. When this Buddha world is displayed, at the same time many other universes are displayed also.

It is like the jewelled net of Indra. In each knot there is a jewel and each jewel reflects all other jewels. In turn, all other jewels reflect this one jewel. Not only that, but all the reflections of each other are reflected in infinity.

If we look at our faces, they are made up of eyes, nose, ears, etc. In themselves these features are all very different from each other. If they combine well together, we might say the face is pretty, but we cannot say that the nose is prettier, or the eyes. Furthermore, the whole face has its own function and each component in turn has its own function. The nose smells, etc. Yet when you see one part, the eyes, for example, you cannot but see the face. By seeing one part you also see the whole.

In the *Avatamsaka* there are the 10 perfections and in the Mahayana there are the six perfections. It is good to cultivate all of them. However, if you practise only one very well, it is the same as practising them all. Through something you do very well you are able to bring the whole sublime universe into existence.

# 3

# The Creative Life

# 11

## uncovering the light
### Yahne Le Toumelin

Yahne Le Toumelin is a French surrealist painter whose
pictures are full of colours and shifting shapes. She is also a
Tibetan Buddhist nun. Yahne has a great sense of humour and
does not take herself seriously, often making puns which are
impossible to translate. However, she is a devoted practitioner
and has done many year-long meditation retreats.

I have been a Buddhist nun since 1968. This was my personal
'68 revolution. To be a Buddhist nun, for me, means first non-
action – 'nun-action'. It is like the light behind; it is non-existence. I find it wonderful being a nun.

Before I became a nun I always secretly hoped I would fall in
love, but I found my amorous life extremely unsatisfactory
because my main love was the search for truth, the true meaning of life. As soon as I abandoned seduction and became a nun
my life became more effective, thus letting go has borne fruits.

If we try to free ourselves from emotions yet want to be
happy emotionally, it is contradictory, because the emotions are
the source of suffering. I cultivated my emotions because in
addition to being an artist I was a sensuous woman. So I gave
myself much suffering.

Now my suffering is totally different: it is the suffering of
others – but I have not resolved this. In Tibet they say if a match
can burn a whole forest, a good thought can open a paradise for
others. I am convinced that peace on Earth depends on us.

We have a treasure, our nature, and we can awaken to its
happiness and harmony. To see this treasure we need to dissolve what is hiding it, like negative emotions and concepts. For
the dissolution of suffering we have to liberate ourselves from
the causes of suffering: attachment, emotions, thoughts, opinions. It is simple, but not easy.

The day I became a nun I gained a discipline, a vow. I lost all
hope in the conventional delusory world by ordaining, but I
gained a great freedom and joy. It is a powerful initiation; taking
the vow is an extraordinary gift and the lineage is pure since the
Buddha. However, I did not take the vow not to paint, as I can
very easily stop painting and just as easily take it up again.

I am not at the stage of non-meditation, though I suppose
actually there is nothing to meditate on. So I meditate to have

stability in non-meditation. My advice to people, as to myself, is to continue to meditate till the day you have no illusions anymore about reality.

## The Light of the Lama

The meditation is on the lama, but the lama is not a person. It is the radiance, the light and the space of the lama. It is all we discover thanks to them, and of course we need purification in order to discover something behind the impurities of the veils of ignorance.

When I said, a little in jest, there is nothing to meditate on, it is because our illusions fade, the space becomes more open and clear, more limitless. When I speak about the sky, the most important thing in the sky is the clarity necessary for the radiance of the sun.

The compassion of the lama enables you to feel universal compassion because they are not a person and neither are you. Devotional practice to the lama is like the sun in the sky; it is the compassion in voidness or the voidness at the heart of compassion. We have a connection with the living lama and have spiritual power through this. If we have a friend or lover, it is that person who reveals to us the feelings of friendship or love, its greatness, its possibility, its energy.

There exists a personal unique lama and when we find this person, we find them in all realized beings. They are the same. However, there is one towards whom we have the most gratitude because it is that person who takes the trouble to guide us and help us purify ourselves. The teaching of the lama is their presence. Looking at my teacher, it is above all that he is. He teaches what he is and he is what he teaches. We can recognize authentic masters through their teachings, actions and presence.

We do not need to have blind faith. The master reveals our own essence to us and an experience of it. As soon as we experience it we ask more of him and as he is limitless, the path is open. It is the inner master who is revealed thanks to the external master. If we were realized we would not need an external teacher as we would already have this inner teacher. We would not even need a master. Realization is an auto-lama!

We really need someone who is like a midwife, doctor or gardener, but the gardener is neither the soil nor the seed. We as the seed are full of potential, but the lama facilitates our awakening to the sun and the rain, so our blossoming can happen, and to blossom is the meaning of the seed, its realization and happiness.

## A Blessing

What is a blessing? It is an inner, mysteriously complete, blossomed happiness, a loving space at ease, an inner freshness and openness for which we feel gratitude to the lama. If you feel this with someone, of course you prefer it to suffering and anguish. I have been a painter, a mother and terribly anguished, but thanks to meeting Tibetan masters and receiving their blessings, this has changed.

It is not with good conceptual intentions that one paints a good picture, so when a new form comes to me I make an offering. These creative urges are completely spontaneous and I offer them. I offer a clean earth, a clean seed which will eventually become a flower, that is, a painting. Instead of painting the light, I have tried to live it; for light, like fire, is the symbol of life.

Myself, I have not made this painting. I offer blue with a rhythmic technique for the love of offering and it displays itself in various forms. This is the painting. If someone likes it, all the better. Some people like lemon tart, others don't. In the end it is as simple as that. If it is your mother who made this lemon tart, you can feel her loving energy in it; thus you establish a connection with those who are touched by that energy.

## Uncovering the Light

At the Uffizi Gallery in Florence, 80 per cent of the paintings are *marouflés* where the paper is glued. This paper is usually white. White is light. The light is behind and it is in removing paint that one uncovers the light. The Germans made studio secrets out of this, but I found the same effects naturally. My technique gives me special possibilities with light. When I discovered this it was like discovering *chou*-cream and, being very hungry, one eats a lot.

Turner used to remove paint a lot with rags. At one time Degas locked himself in his studio to make monotypes [a unique print taken from a glass or metal plate] because he had discovered that by removing paint there were extraordinary effects of light. German painting liberated me and maybe unconsciously I was influenced by Max Ernst, who in his last years also discovered these techniques. I discovered how to do it by removing paint and finding the light behind, from underneath, by revealing the play of white in the paper. It is often exactly the opposite of what we learned in academic schools where one plays with shades and adds white to make light.

I make my woof, the woof that suits me that day. Then on this frame I add paint with one hand with the brush and remove it with the other hand. All my Impressionist side – the side of painting which I adore like Rembrandt, Turner, Monet – I add, and then I remove it and that is the side of the Germans, the sixteenth-century painters Albrecht Altdorfer and Matthias Grünewald.

This technique corresponds to what I am looking for spiritually. It is by removing, dissolving, melting that the light appears. This gesture is a fantastic symbol. The technique fixes me in one way, but appeals to me immensely because it reveals so much light. It is magical. I surprise myself, going from surprise to surprise, from wonder to wonder. It is astonishing what luminous phenomena my technique opens up.

It is an apparitional style of painting. Many things appear in my paintings, but there is no need to let them dominate. It is a little like surfing; I need to maintain balance. There is a sort of dialogue where I try not to fall into duality.

## One Form, One Light

When you work on a painting on an easel, there is an object you copy in the classical manner. There is all of art history contemplating you behind your back and then the painting in front of you. Personally, I work horizontally. As I paint, things appear and I become one with the wave, with the apparition. I am surprised and amused. It is a revelation for me each time.

There is a search for purest light in my paintings. Often there is only one form. I owe this to an important art dealer, René Drouin, who had faith in my painting. He told me that since I had such a wealth of imagination I should try the discipline of one form, one asceticism, one colour. For about two years I tried this in a painting retreat.

The simplest forms are the circle and the square. Often my image is nearly a square. It is so fine that there are several veils. The light is behind and you see a veil, another one and again another one. I also call them 'mirrors' because I like what Marguerite Porète wrote about 'the mirror of the simple souls annihilated'. The mirror has a certain luminous apparition. In religious literature there are many mirrors: in Talmudism, Sufism, Tibetan Buddhism. It is a rich analogy.

I would like to render homage to Marguerite Porète, who was burnt by French priests on the Place de l'Hotel de Ville in Paris in 1310 because she wrote a manuscript about a soul high in the mountains above the winds. This text is truly extraordinary and very similar to my research. Paris should pay homage to Marguerite because they burnt her with her manuscript. However a copy was saved. Her descriptions of the soul are beautiful.

When Eskimos want to express something they place a stone in a certain way and form a pattern. These stones are called *inuchnuk*. Once a Japanese curator was very touched when he saw some, so he transported them to his museum. When they arrived all people saw was a pile of stones and they thought the curator had gone mad. Then he put them back together as the Eskimos would have done and it was very beautiful.

Every day, even if I have done baroque painting, very loaded, I end by doing one sole light, by setting down one *inuchnuk*. No one light is similar to another, though I have done hundreds of them. The simplest image of light expresses something. It is as if men lay down a stone, an *inuchnuk*, and women a light. There is such transparency I cannot go further, otherwise there is nothing anymore. Sometimes I add another plane of light like a sword, then an outline of a wave. There is movement, an enormous amount of life, but it is veiled by the ultimate light.

## The Drop

There are two movements. First is filling in paint. It is like a dance. When I take it away, it is also like a dance. I do not take it away in one movement, as we would let a curtain fall down, but gradually. This is gestural painting, but it could be called abstract, visionary or fantastic. I do not care about the professional designation; my painting can be baroque and classical, static or dynamic.

In my recent paintings there are mirrors like windows which open, like tides, a whole life which cascades like birds in flight. Victor Hugo said angels are celestial cities, birds of the suburbs. In some of my paintings you see angels in the foreground and birds in flight. They are vibrations of lines and colours, in fact, of the space. The sun reflects itself in these mirrors. I try to remove the salt of the vastness without losing its flavour. This vastness is like the ocean which feeds the saltpans and gives salt to humanity. I lived for a long time in such a landscape.

In 1978 I did a whole series of paintings inspired by Talièsin. He was a Celtic bard who wrote many beautiful poems. A great part of my inspiration comes from the spiritual path of the Celtic legends. There is one which says: 'a hundred thousand years at the tip of my sword'. This has inspired me a lot.

Once I painted a tryptich to represent the Grail. It had a matrix of light with a drop. One finds a lot of drops in my painting. This is also a very old idea. When the Dead Sea Scrolls were discovered, I noticed that the first Christians called grace 'the drop': 'It will come as an autumn rain on the dried out earth of our hearts.' It is the marriage of sky and earth, the original cell.

When I went to Darjeeling, I saw jewels that were just like drops. I had brought a drop of crystal to my teacher. The Nyingmapas talk about the drop of the heart. All this made me burn with enthusiasm for the drop.

## Painting a Spiritual Language

I pay a lot of attention to the drop, the celestial matrix and transparency; they are a language. I also paint a lot of palaces. Once for the choreographer Maurice Bejart I did 120 metres [394 ft] of palaces, crystalline palaces which opened onto doors of light with flights of angels and oceans of light unfurling. I have a special technique for creating the sea. I am an ocean when I paint it.

Recently I was asked to do something for Handel's *Messiah*. I wanted to do something big – a matrix of light, oceans of light, lots of flights and lights. It is like a spiritual vocabulary, without end. I have made thousands of angels at the tip of my sword.

There are also many golden mountains in visionary art. I find these ideas in the spiritual writings of the great fourteenth-century nuns Hildegard of Bingen and Hordewich of Anvers. They speak of oceans of light, crystal palaces and doors which open into paradise. However, nowadays the hells are more in fashion than paradise.

## Rainbows and Melting Colours

My interest in the appearances of painted forms and the spiritual life is similar. When I was young I was already asking a lot of questions. I thought God was a circle and I drew forms in relation to metaphysical problems. Finally I did an MA in philosophy while becoming a painter. I went to studios and I drew and drew.

At 17 I had already copied hundreds of classics. I did portraits of all my friends and also landscapes. I was a classical painter then. But one day in my teacher's studio something happened – I saw only rainbows, melting colours, and I painted this vision. But my teacher, Mac Avoy, only told me I needed vitamins (it was during the war). So someone told me to go to the artist André L'hote, who, on the contrary, showed me off, but as he did not correct me finally I learned nothing. He always exclaimed in front of my paintings as he found them ideal.

## Faster, Faster

Finally I realized this was modern art. Then I discovered Gurdjieff, who made me draw faster and faster. He used to say to me it was Huedia yoga. He always made me draw, telling me: 'Faster, faster!' Drawing like this helped me a little to discover my quick technique.

I have also painted very classically, like Bosch and Bruegel – fantastic and weird things, *a tempera*. I learned this mainly in Mexico with one of Max Ernst's partners, Leonora Carrington.

We wanted to go to Tibet together as our friendship was also spiritual. She was an amazing woman, truly surrealist, who had occult powers and was creative in all her activities. She mentioned me to the surrealist André Breton, telling him I was a sort of magician, so Breton made a long journey to see me, but also because he wanted to hear about Gurdjieff. There was a mysterious aura, a little cheap and showy, around Gurdjieff at that time.

In the end I painted without a teacher, although I remembered Gurdjieff and how to work fast. I worked in Paris for many years, but put too much hope into my work, wishing to find the truth of appearances in painting. These were horrible years because it all finished in anguish and despair. I feel truly sorry for painters because there is nothing to find. Appearances are not deep at all.


## Liberation of the Heart

Fortunately I was reading the mystics, the Dead Sea Scrolls and so on. Every evening I had visions. I was seeing palaces, mountains, angels. My paintings mirrored what I was living. Finally I did an exhibition in February 1968. There was already a little of May '68 in the air. My theme was 'to liberate the creative imagination', and I did many great banners which were replicated during the days of May '68.

This exhibition is bonded to my spiritual life and was the first to succeed. It gave me money and on the last day of the exhibition I went to Darjeeling in India. The manifesto of my exhibition had been: 'Long live the revolution of the heart.' I took a small Breton silver heart for my teacher's wife in India. At once she put the heart with the pointed end on top. This was the revolution of the heart. Then Kangyur Rinpoche told me that there are some yogis who have hearts with the pointed end on top. It was this kind of meeting which galvanized me, because for me the heart was often like a mountain and I painted it with the pointed end on top too.

When I arrived in Darjeeling I was wearing a round mirror with a spiral on it round my neck. I asked Rinpoche what this corresponded to. He replied: 'To nothing at all.' I cried. Twenty years of studying the spiral and the mirror and all this meant nothing! So I accepted to willingly go beyond all the symbols I had concocted from the spiritual Parisian life.

I remained in Darjeeling and for seven years I did not paint. I had gone beyond the space of my painting. I abandoned my daubings without regret, but most of all Parisian life, the artistic life. Finally I was completely disconnected from it.

## Like Baking a Cake

I came back to France in 1975 when our teacher died and lived at the Château of Chaban in the Dordogne. We received many Tibetan teachers there. For several years I devoted myself to cooking for these teachers.

One day Dudjom Rinpoche remarked that I did not seem to paint anymore. He had noticed many of my paintings in our friends' houses. I told him I did not know how to paint after seven years without painting. He replied: 'In the same way as you are cooking.' I thought, 'Why not? If one does something well, if one cooks well, making nice cakes, why not paint in the same way?'

So I started painting again. While cooking for Dudjom Rinpoche I did 30 paintings in 30 days, completely inspired by this master. It was extraordinary.

By now, I knew not to grasp at the appearances of the paintings anymore. In the same way I tried not to grasp at people.

In 1979 I was asked to do a one woman show at the Grand Palais, which professionally was very interesting. I was waking up with an inspiration of paradise every day. Sometimes it is said that a painter 'is on the motif'; for me at this time it was an unlimited motif. Each of my paintings failed compared to what I was seeing and feeling, but this made them a little better than usual. All my paintings from that moment on were failures. Each time I painted I wanted to confess my ignorance. It was like saying: 'Here is the cake!' and some people liking the cake and some not. Some people were moved by the energy which lives in my paintings; for example, Master Deshimaru used to say there was chi in them.

## Paintings of Joy

Nowadays, from time to time I do not paint. When I did a four-year retreat I did not paint at all and did not miss it.

When I started to paint anew I met Maurice Bejart again at the anniversary of the French Revolution at the Grand Palais. He said; 'Why don't you do an image of joy? You must long to do something like that.' Of course it poured out of me like a waterfall. He let me use the Grand Palais and I had it all to myself for a weekend.

For two years I painted hundreds of pictures, paintings of joy. I cannot explain them, they just came out like that. They are not traditional paintings at all. Reading Shintao's treatises on Chinese painting I finally found a connection with the Chinese who painted mountains and water, yin and yang.

## A Marvellous Recipe

There is a programme of long meditation retreats in the Nyingmapa school, a marvellous recipe which unfolds in a closed space, with many blessings and energy. The aim is awakening, freedom and the possibility of saying a word of truth, of lying less. It is impossible to define illumination, but our path towards it is developed through all sorts of techniques, prayers, studies and yogas, with the yoga of the mind of course being the main one in all of them.

Since we receive many initiations during the retreat there are certain practices we continue to do every day afterwards. As long as we have not achieved meditative stability it is in our interest to have the support of being faithful to practices, recitations and visualizations. As for me, I am not at a level where I do not need to practise anymore; I am not a dzogchenpa living my life perfectly, spontaneously.

## A Profusion of Appearances

My teacher, Tulku Pema Wangyal, does not pass judgement on my painting. He never comments on appearances, but simply lets me express these phenomena, which is not the same as realizing their dream or vacuity. The vacuity is not what I imagined it to be. It is not a void which is additional to the appearances. It would be easier to qualify it simply as impermanence, the profusion and abundance of appearances, of manifestations which arise and pass, ephemeral and inconstant.

The Dalai Lama nowadays talks about fullness and plenitude, and in Bhutan people often learn to read from the *Prajnaparamita Sutra* which states: 'Form is emptiness.' However, they have an exuberant creativity in dance, sculpture and offering. In their lives is generosity, a fullness of forms completely unlimited. What a generous vacuity! Whereas people who think forms are solid are completely rigid, like Western artists. It is a yoke. When a painter finds a form they cannot escape from it anymore; they are caught, frozen. There was an exhibition of some tryptichs in the Louvre – canvases, one black, one white and one grey. One cannot do this for centuries. How boring!

For me creativity is the natural state. Freeing the natural state, we free 'the original kindness'. At the source, which is the present moment, there is a potential, a possibility which only asks to bloom, an opening, a space.

Often people do not understand when they see my exuberances. They do not see how it can come from somebody who has undergone a spiritual search. They imagine my work will be bare. I am not really appreciated by people who have applied Zen to a lack of ornamentalism, which seems to me to be a draining, a drying out. For me, on the contrary, voidness, dissolution, is an ocean of joy. It is not a desert where there is not even sand.

## A Sense of Space

I was also influenced by my friendship with the painters Pierre Soulages and Georges Mathieu. I very much admired the freedom they took with gesture, after Jackson Pollock. They were opposites from the point of view of conception and creation. Soulages used to say that Mathieu had an emotive gesture, whilst Soulages had gestures of presence.

I learned a sense of and a great openness to freedom from them. When they saw my paintings they said: 'Why don't you paint big?' I went to Brittany where I had a studio in a large house. I found the largest surface I could [sheets of adhesive vinyl] and put them on the floor. It was wonderful; I had finally found a space which corresponded with what I wanted to express. I put this sense of space in my canvases.

The painter's space is often talked about. When it is a representational work, one sees a small boat on the horizon line. When it is a gestural painting, it can be a space without reference to dimensions or concepts like the musical space.

There are people who have an inner space even though they might not be painters. I felt this when I met the photographer Henri Cartier-Bresson at L'hote's studio. Suddenly I saw someone with space. He gave it in photos. He gives it in painting now. He is a libertarian, a revolutionary. People who have space are inevitably revolutionary because they go beyond references.

## Running after Clouds

When I was a child, busy with my schoolbooks, I already wanted to go to Tibet, having read the books of Alexandra David-Neel, the traveller and writer on Tibet. It was my dream, my obsession. I was unhappy and uncomfortable in my education, although my parents were kind, charming and gave me everything. Everything was perfect from their point of view, only I was unhappy not to be somewhere I could realize something deeper than what was being offered to me, than what I was finding. I searched. I went to the Dominicans, but this was unsatisfying; in those days you were criticized if you read Master Eckhart.

In 1968 it was my good fortune to enter into Buddhism. I felt I did not deserve such happiness, and it has gone beyond all my hopes and visions. When I met my Tibetan teacher for the first time, he was radiating voidness, which I was not sure about, and the love I was looking for, universal like the sun. Until then I had run after clouds.

## A Blue Line

Many of my early paintings are expressionist and full of suffering. I feel sorry to have painted them. They are all I do not like in painting, sad and useless at the same time. This generally leads to suicide or madness, like Van Gogh and Nicolas de Stael. I escaped it, but it does not please me to see wasted transparencies. It was a prison really, like doing time. I cannot like those paintings, as they are not paintings of love. They are paintings of suffering, which does not bring anything to anybody.

Now I try to paint naturally. You can radiate the natural state everywhere. You can even emanate kindness in painting. Before I was fretting and anxious, so the form of the cross informed me while I was working furiously on my canvas. There is so much painting like this, from Soutines to our contemporaries. They tear their paintings and people say it is the end of manual painting. Gestural painting is not obliged to be like boxing, aggressive. It can be harmony between heaven and Earth, a dance like tai-chi.

One day I made a blue line on a painting. I found it fantastic. A doctor saw it the same day, bought it and went away with it. I was happy to have sold it. The next day I did another blue line, but I have never done such a blue line as that again.

# 12
## the struggle to succeed
## Pang Kwihi

Pang Kwihi is a Korean Buddhist writer with a beautiful and
expressive face who is handicapped and in a wheelchair
because her lower body did not develop. She is a successful
novelist, Buddhist lecturer and scriptwriter. Originally she
wanted to become a doctor, but in the 1970s it was difficult for
handicapped people to go to university and she was refused
entrance to medical college because of her handicap. She
turned towards Tongguk Buddhist University, not because she
wanted to study Buddhism, but who would accept her
determined which university and course she attended.

## Dealing with Difficulties

I started the study of Buddhism without faith in it. I had had no contact with it because I could not go to the temples, thus could not meet monks or nuns, although my mother was a diligent Buddhist and visited the temples regularly. When I began to study I realized Buddhism was a philosophy which could be very helpful, and I became attracted to it and its religious practices.

I try to apply Buddhist tenets in my daily life. Often I meet difficulties, but then I think of something the Buddha said which helps me to handle them. For example, if I look at the eightfold path, there is right speech. Why right speech? On meeting people, I understand why it is necessary to use the right words and the right way of saying them, because of how people might perceive and react to what I say.

It is also important to use right effort, the philosophy of the middle way and the truth about the three poisons [greed, hatred and ignorance]; all these are very useful in everyday life. The Buddhist teachings have become a guide, a source. When I react in a certain way, I reflect that this is why the Buddha gave different kinds of advice.

## The Blind Disciple

Among Korean Buddhists there is often the attitude that if someone is ill, handicapped or has serious difficulties, it is because of misdeeds in a past life. This makes us feel we are at fault for being disabled; consequently many disabled people dislike Buddhism. Among handicapped people in Korea there is a definite rejection of Buddhism because of the theory of karmic retribution.

Yet the more we have difficulty and handicaps, the more we feel the need for religion and are religiously inclined. If 40 per cent of ordinary people are religious, 80 per cent of the handi-capped will be religious. Among these, 4 per cent will be Buddhists, 88 per cent Protestants and the rest will be Catholics. Of the 4 per cent, it does not always mean they are believers, but that their mother goes to the temple.

However, I look at this in a different way. In Buddha's time, in Indian society there was already the idea of reincarnation and karma from past lives. This idea was incredibly strong, it stuck and has come down all the way to the present day. It was not invented by the Buddha, it was already there in Indian cul-ture and so the Buddhists just adopted it in order to make themselves understood and acceptable to that society. All schol-ars agree about this.

The Buddha did not emphasize karmic retribution, that we pay in this life for our past lives' misdeeds. He was not too pre-occupied with the body and its meaning; actually he said we should practise in spite of it and not be so concerned with it.

For my talks I look for stories and teachings in the Buddhist canon which are relevant to disabled people. Among the 10 great disciples of the Buddha there was Anayuli, who was blind. He lost his sight not because of misdeeds in his past life, but because of wanting to practise the Buddhadharma so much he practised day and night tirelessly and became blind. The Buddha said that Anayuli had obtained the wisdom eye – that although he could not see with his physical eyes, he could see with his mind's eye, he had achieved that kind of strength in his practice. The Buddha praised him highly and he was one of his most celebrated disciples.

In Buddha's time, his disciples begged and sewed their own robes out of rags. Anayuli could not see to thread the needle so the Buddha came to do it for him. In this way the Buddha was respectful and kind to the disabled, and in the sutras there are many examples and instances like this. I am thinking of gather-ing this kind of material together and making a book from it.

## What Is the Greater Unhappiness?

In 1988, the Olympic Games were held in Seoul, accompanied by the Handicapped Olympics. People became conscious of the needs of handicapped people and interested in their welfare, and I started to give dharma talks to groups of handicapped people. I also give lectures about Buddhist social welfare to people who are interested in the subject, as I wrote my thesis on it.

I try to give the handicapped a better understanding of reincarnation and karmic retribution, and endeavour to present the Buddha and his teaching in a way that is helpful and inspiring for them.

The Buddha became a mendicant because of suffering and his desire to transcend suffering. He realized there was something lacking, so he renounced the world and became a mendicant. I respect this in him. He had everything – money, respect, abilities – and lacked nothing outwardly. However, his troubles were spiritual and started with the death of his mother. I found this very convincing and it is a story with which we can identify ourselves. Nowadays, there is still the unhappiness of people who have money and abilities; then there is also the unhappiness of people like us who are poor or limited in their ability. Truly, what is the greater unhappiness? I reflect upon this often. Buddhism has a lot to offer because it presents a solution and practical methods to get at the root of unhappiness and suffering.

One of the greatest sufferings is conflict. However rich we have become, however many material things we amass, these do not resolve this kind of suffering. In a way riches make the distance between us and happiness even greater. What is the true reason for unhappiness? If we study Buddhism and apply it, we realize that true happiness can be cultivated and this helps us to lead a more contented life.

## Meditation Is Not Just Sitting Still

Meditation is not just sitting still. It is difficult to sit cross legged or bow to the Buddha if you are disabled. In the Christian Church there is no special bodily way of praying, it is enough to pray, but in Buddhism we have to bow or sit in meditation in certain definite postures. These ritualistic forms present a difficulty for disabled people and put an obstacle between the disabled and the spiritual world. We must find ways in Buddhism to make meditation and praying accessible to all.

It is essential to go back to the basis of Buddha's life and his original teaching. Without any special form, we can read a few lines of a sutra in the morning so as not to forget its message and apply its meaning throughout the day. For example, today I should be mindful and not utter thoughtless words, reckless remarks. Even if there were to arise a situation where I would be tempted to make such remarks, I should restrain myself and be patient.

If we leave home with such an intention, even if we have to discuss something with someone who is difficult, we will keep to our intention, maintain peace of mind and not hurt the other person. We thus endeavour to actualize Buddhism in our life. It could be enough to keep the five precepts. If we were to keep even one precept per month, our behaviour would surely transform swiftly.

## We Are Equal

I write scripts for the radio, essays or short stories for disabled magazines or Buddhist magazines and a book once a year. My books are not specialized and I am very interested in literature. When I think about life, its meaning and difficulty, I make a link with literature. I have written about 10 books, most of them novels, but I only write about subjects connected to Buddhism or disabled people.

I wrote a novel called *Rahula* which was popular and widely read. Rahula was the son of the Buddha and the meaning of his name is 'handicap'. In this book, I investigated what things restrain and bind people in their lives and what things liberate them. How do they act when bound and when liberated? They are bound, then liberated, then bound again; I explored that movement in my novel.

There are many writers among the handicapped, not because they are more gifted at it, but because this is one of the few things they can do. There are people who spend their whole day sitting or lying, people who cannot go out at all, but they can write and express what they have in their minds and hearts. I created the Association of Disabled Writers to make them known and to find publishers for their writing. We have also put together a literature magazine.

I do this work because I like it, also because it is distressing that the attitude of Korean people towards disabled people does not change. Living standards have risen, people have become well off and sometimes they give a certain amount of money to handicapped people. But this is not enough; it is only when they see disabled people as equal human beings that this will be true welfare. It is important to change the attitude and thinking of people towards the disabled, and a lot of my work is trying to gain recognition for the disabled from Korean people.

## Our Appearance Is Not Important

I saw a programme on TV about people who have strange facial features. They can walk, hear and speak, and have everything functioning perfectly. However, just because their faces are different from those of other people, they cannot function in society. At school they are ridiculed so they cannot go; at work they are not accepted and are given a hard time. When I heard this, I thought it was so sad. It made me wonder why our bodies and our appearance in society are so important.

This is why it is essential for the Buddha's teachings to be made widely known because the Buddha said that outside appearances are not important. What is important is the mind, the thoughts we carry inside.

It is important to help people become more open-minded, more accepting of differences and less discriminating. Otherwise much pain is created just because one's skin, one's face or one's body is different from that of other people. The Buddha himself said: 'Do not have a mind which makes discrimination.' When we meet an unknown person, we perceive that person with a discriminating mind, but there is no need for this; all humans are the same.

I always try to put this belief into practice. Sometimes, of course, I wonder and judge too: 'Has this person studied a lot or not?' When I become aware of these thoughts I remind myself of my intention and change such discriminating thinking at once.

# 13
## zen and the art of painting
## Okbong Sunim

Okbong Sunim is a very old Korean nun who is a Zen painter.
Over the years she has held many exhibitions and a book of her
paintings has recently been published. She is quite
handicapped by arthritis, though she is very lively and
friendly. She lives in a small flat in Seoul.

## Painting is Meditation

Painting is meditation for me. As soon as I pick up the brush, there is no difference from meditation. However many distracted thoughts might want to arise, there is no place for them when I paint. My mind is empty of distractions and there is only the painting being painted. It is meditation because there is only one thought. If one has meditated holding a *hwadu*, one realizes that painting and holding a *hwadu* are not two different things. Holding a *hwadu* and holding the intention to paint in one's mind and painting are the same.

As in the nunnery, here too in this flat, I wake up naturally at 3 a.m. After washing my face and brushing my teeth, I sit in meditation. After that I eat breakfast and go about my daily activities. In the evening it is quiet, so I chant and do some more meditation.

Sometimes I paint all day; in a way it is as if I were meditating all day. I am so focused that often I do not realize the whole day has gone by. If I am too tired I cannot paint, but if I am less tired, then I pick up the brush. If someone asks me to teach them, then I teach.

## Maintain Your Intention

When I teach students, I start with the basics. People these days are talented, so they understand quickly and can apply the instructions easily, but what I find disappointing is that they have little endurance. If you start something, you must endeavour to finish it. If you pick up a brush you should push on and on, trying again and again. Painting the 'four gracious plants' [orchid, bamboo, plum blossom and chrysanthemum] is difficult and when something is difficult you should advance by trying repeatedly. Putting in effort is important. Nowadays people just try a little and then give up. This is called 'good beginning and a dull finish'. At the beginning I ask them: 'Will you do this till you are 60 or 70?' and they say: 'Yes.' However, after a while they always find various reasons to stop. They are too busy, or this or that.

As painter and artist you must maintain the mind you started with, even if you do not hold the brush every day. Each week, you need to hold the brush for 10 to 20 minutes every evening, if possible, painting on old newspapers, as a game. If you do this, then it is always with you and it will take hold. It is not necessary to practise for long periods of time. Even in the midst of attending to your affairs, in your mind you should not let go of your intention and your awareness of painting.

## Compose Your Mind

Let the mind be quiet and focused. You cannot paint if your mind is noisy and complicated. The mind must be calm and composed. Start painting after having meditated for a few minutes to compose and calm the mind. If your mind is calm there is no reason for the painting not to work. Everything comes from the mind. Everything is the mind. So the painting too is the mind. If the mind is noisy and restless, the painting will be noisy and restless. The mind is one. 'All the dharmas return to the one' is just as it is.

Buddhism is about what appears naturally, about awakening to our nature, and a painting is an expression of ourselves, of our temperament. Each artist displays, just as it is, their own character. When we produce a work out of quietness, we show the quiet, a place where there is neither I nor you.

If a work comes out of our one-pointedness, it shows one-pointedness. For example, if the mind is deep, quiet and calm, then how is the *hwadu*? The *hwadu* is brightly 'What is it?'. If at that time you take hold of the brush and paint, you are painting with one-pointedness.

## The Four Gracious Plants

When I was young I enjoyed calligraphy and studied with a good teacher. I started to learn painting when I was 15. What I do is not totally Eastern, nor is it Western. It is what is called the 'four gracious plants': orchid, bamboo, plum blossom and chrysanthemum. I have been painting these all my life.

The four gracious plants have a lot of meaning. If you paint an orchid, even in one leaf there is integrity and purpose. It represents nature and is also very beautiful. There is a special kind of orchid; if it were here, the whole room would be filled with its perfume and someone could even smell it outside. The orchid displays beauty, nature and fragrance all by itself, without caring for approval or disapproval.

The bamboo is straight and green, and always stays the same. It never changes its straightness or its greenness. Whether it is hot and sunny or cold and snowy, it is always the same. Of the four gracious plants it has the most strength and character. The bamboo was also used for making flutes long ago as it gave the best sound.

The plum blossom is special because it blooms on bare branches at the end of winter, even in the snow, when there is no leaf, no green or colour anywhere. The constancy of the plum blossom is great. However cold it might be, it will blossom.

The chrysanthemum is special because it comes after all the other flowers have finished in autumn and blooms after the first frost of early winter.

So these four gracious plants all have their individual characteristics and are symbolic of beauty, constancy and integrity.

When I was young I lived in an area where there were four famous painters. One of them told me not to restrict myself to the four gracious plants and to paint mountains and rivers also. However, I thought the plants were enough.

Actually it requires a lot of strength to draw the four gracious plants. You may only see a black ink drawing and think it looks easy, but every single leaf has to be alive; if it is dead, the picture does not work. Leaf by leaf, each must be alive, and this is why it is worth doing. People gifted in painting the four gracious plants are quite rare. When I studied with my teacher, five of us started, but I am the only one who stayed with it.

## Painting Again

I became a nun in my mid-thirties and am now 80 years old. When I became a nun I had already been painting for some years. It was after liberation from the Japanese occupation, which was followed by the Korean War. Korea used to be one country, then was divided into North and South at the end of the Second World War, then the North invaded the South and this turned into the Korean War. There was a lot of killing and misery, even Koreans killing each other. I was horrified to see this and started to dislike living in a world where this could happen.

When the war ended, the country was divided in two by a demarcation line. I did not want to live even one more day in such a world, so I became a nun in Tongkaksa, a sutra study hall. I decided to practise meditation, threw my paint brushes away and went to various meditation halls.

A few years later, after staying a few meditation seasons at Soknamsa [a Zen nunnery near Pusan in the southern part of South Korea], my knees started to ache very badly. It was so bad I could not bow or sit and could barely walk. I came to Seoul to receive some treatment, for which I needed money. During my days as a nun I had not cared about money at all, but now I needed some. So friends suggested that I mount an exhibition of my paintings.

So it was because of my illness that I started to paint again. I put all my effort into it and painted many pictures which were exhibited successfully. After the exhibition, I hoped to be cured and wanted to go back to the mountains to meditate. But my legs did not really heal and my back was also painful. I felt a little better from the treatment, but it did not cure my condition.

I also had a disciple who had been with me since she left elementary school and I had to stay in Seoul to help her with her study. Now she is in university. I felt that since she was my responsibility I had to take good care of her education. These days it is necessary for the young nuns to be taught and to learn things. So I stayed here in Seoul, day by day, month by month, and I am here still. Four years ago a newspaper sponsored a full exhibition of my paintings. At first I said I could not do one anymore, but finally I agreed.

## The Artist

An artist must paint pictures and I cannot not do it. When I am ill, I take up the *hwadu*. When I am a little better, I feel I must paint. Then I forget everything else, distracted thoughts and all. So the painting and I become one. Even if I intend to do something else, I cannot; I forget everything and everything rests naturally.

Artists have a distinct temperament, whatever they are working on. Because of this, it is easy to misunderstand them, but truly there must be something in them to do smart and intelligent work. If someone is dim and vague and does dim and vague things, they will not stand out.

Sometimes you might wonder: 'Why is this person behaving like this?' You cannot understand and do not know. Often artists say to each other, 'This painting is not coming along well.' By evening their head aches, they get angry and shout, and finally go out. 'Why are you going out?' one might ask. 'The painting is not going well,' the other replies. But if it always turned out well, it would not do, it would have no value. There is value only when in the midst of it not working well, one suddenly ascends to a higher standard. This becomes art. Whatever artist one is, whatever method one uses, when it comes down to the state of mind required to produce art, it is all the same.

# 4

# Healing the World

# 14
## songs are flowers of the mind
### Jongmok Sunim

Jongmok Sunim is an extraordinary young Korean nun who is
a disc jockey on a Buddhist radio station with a programme of
classical music. She also runs another programme helping
those in need. She is a fine singer and sometimes holds
concerts, which are very popular. I saw her compering a
musical afternoon and she was brilliant: funny and spiritual at
the same time.

## Buddhist Radio

I have been in charge of a music programme at the Buddhist radio station for three years. Since I was very young I liked music and was gifted at playing musical instruments and singing. Once I entered the nunnery there was no opportunity to make music, but when the Buddhist radio station was created, I wanted to transmit the dharma and introduce people to music.

Music for me is connected to religious feelings, but not to a definite religion. We have been born and we are living. How should we live? How can we live loving one another? I try to convey these feelings and questions through music. I would like to be a small lamp that illuminates, and I see music as a skilful means by which I can convey how to have love and compassion for other people.

Master Bojo said Buddhist chants are recitations which come from deep within the Buddha's mind. They are not simply repetitions of words. He said these words of the people are flowers of the mind and the fruits of the mind are songs. Singing expresses that the flowers have already blossomed and now the fruits are ripening.

Songs are not only the sounds made by a certain person. Chanting is the vocal expression of the mind which intends to become Buddha.

## Meeting the Buddha through Music

I organize musical meetings in temple grounds because I like to show beautiful music to music lovers. I want to show Buddhist laypeople that inside a monastery, a place where the Buddha is, it is not only by praying and chanting that you can meet the Buddha, but also through classical music. The Buddha always manifests in the midst of a happy, appreciative mind.

I am very pleased with the musical meetings; they help people experience a great joy. Buddhists can learn about music; also, between numbers I give a few words of explanation about the sutras.

I try to convey the message of the Buddha, not only in the words of the Buddha but also in the words of Jesus, Confucius and Socrates. Buddha is the teacher who lived 2,500 years ago in India, but throughout time there have been many people who have tried to live like him. Through the example of these people, I too hope to walk the same path of wisdom and compassion. By hearing about these people's experiences we can reflect about life and ponder on the best way to live.

In everyday life I would like to give people something which can make them joyful and happy, which can make them share love.

## A Breath of Fresh Air

In our courtyard at home there was a tree. In winter its leaves would curl, fall and shrivel up. As I watched, I wondered why the leaves of this tree shrivelled and died and I asked my grandmother. She told me everything which is born will die. I have always felt the suffering of birth and death, but they did not teach about this at school and it stifled me. I was searching aimlessly till one day I met some nuns and talked with them. I felt as though a breath of fresh air had passed through me, so I decided to be like them, to cultivate the mind and be of benefit to others.

I have been a nun for 16 years. I was 16 when I was ordained so I was the attendant of an elder, the leader of the meditation hall. Every morning and evening I would sit and she would teach me meditation. She hoped I would live in the world and spread the dharma widely, and encouraged me to teach lay groups all over the country.

As I came in contact with society I realized I needed to study social work, so I went to university. I am interested in social work but I also have an ardent wish to meditate. If I were to spend time sitting quietly in meditation in the mountains, it would help me to understand, to realize my own self. But in a way this is a desire, so I control and restrain it and say to myself: 'Let's live with a mind which always practises amidst people in difficulty.'

## Precepts Are Like a Hedge

The Buddhist precepts are like a hedge. To teach people beneficial actions is difficult, but people act selfishly without being taught. In school or any other training place they tell you again and again to practise good deeds, but it seems hard for people to behave well all the time.

The Buddha never said the precepts were absolute; he did not give them like an order: 'You must do this at all costs!' The precepts are there to help us keep an eye on our behaviour. They encourage us to reflect on our actions in order to improve them through our own volition, and we can use them as a support and an aid in our practice.

If we look at the *vinaya*, we can see the Buddha as a father, thoughtful and kind. We can really feel his humanity, even in the instructions of telling nuns to sit on a cushion when they meditate. Each precept came into being to show what behaviour would be detrimental for ourselves and other people, according to circumstances. He told people not to perform actions which cause suffering. This is the basis of the precepts: not to cause suffering to ourselves or others.

The Buddha mentioned music in connection with the senses. We can easily and quickly lose ourselves in sensations and defilements, then distractions may arise. So the Buddha said monks and nuns should not sing, dance, go to singing or dancing places, wear jewellery or perfume. My intention is not for us hedonistically to enjoy ourselves through the senses, but to experience and practise love through them. Thus music is not an end in itself, but an instrument to bring love into the mind.

A Buddhist text says: 'The precepts are to be open and closed', so it is essential to know when to open the precepts and when to close them. We must be careful not to make them tight or inflexible, otherwise we fall into rigidness. On the other hand, keeping them too loosely, or not keeping them at all and doing just what we want without any reflection, is not the right way either.

## A Buddha Is Kind

Someone asked the Dalai Lama: 'How can an ordinary person know you are a living Buddha?' He replied easily: 'A Buddha is someone who is kind to everyone.' A Buddha is not someone who behaves extraordinarily, who has supernatural powers or who is lofty. On the contrary, living a very ordinary life, as a farmer or a dustman, we can always try to be kind to our neighbours. If we display a kind mind we are endowed with a Bodhisattva's mind and activities.

This is what I want to convey – kindness. People often think religious teachings are too 'high' and difficult. Why is this? Every religion uses a special vocabulary with words that are difficult to understand for ordinary people. However, the Buddha talked in an easy way, using simple words. He talked in a way that all sentient beings could understand and the words he used were the words they used too.

In Zen, we often say 'No birth, no death', but this is extraordinary. Anyone who has a body knows for sure they were born and are going to die and can see it with their own eyes, thus it is hard to believe or understand these words. Only someone who has practised Zen can understand them directly.

Some great monks talk of 'entering directly into Buddhahood by awakening suddenly'. For them there is no gradual path. But ordinary people do not understand this kind of talk, so we explain the meaning to them, helping them to enter the Buddha's path.

## Nothing Is Unique and Peerless

Religions must be careful about claiming to have a unique method that is the only right one. Some say meditation is unique and peerless; others say the Buddha's doctrine is unique and peerless. But there is nothing which is unique and peerless. According to our affinity and karma we take a certain direction, and according to our capacity we practise the Buddhist path. One step at a time, we advance to sit closer to the Buddha.

Often the number of believers in a certain religion is used as proof of the truth of that religion. If a religion has only a few believers it is supposed to have less truth or no truth at all. This is ridiculous – truth is not dependent on the number of believers. What is important is how people practise and realize the teaching of that religion.

Under the influence of some religious leaders, people abandon everything. Recently some teacher announced the end of the world. People believed him and prayed only to be saved on the predicted day, but nothing happened! Thus we can see religions have great power to fool people.

If the light of wisdom shines brightly, a religion is like the sun which illuminates everything, but if we make a mistake, we become like a blind person who might fall and die in an abyss because everything is dark.

Sometimes religions make people fearful by saying they must believe in God or in the Buddha. The Buddha said it is not right for people to believe in a religion in this way. His word directly expressed and transmitted compassion, and Buddhism as a religion is about showing compassion. I respect the Buddha and take him as my teacher, and I want to live according to his teaching of compassion.

## Not a Frog in a Well

Sometimes I answer the phone for our Buddhist on-line phone service, called the Compassion Line. Until recently there was no Buddhist counselling telephone service because a telephone was seen as a machine, with materialistic and mechanistic con-notations. Buddhists have a tendency to see themselves beyond matter. However society is changing, the telephone has become an ordinary part of life and we realize people benefit from tele-phone consultation and counselling.

To prepare for the counselling, for six months I trained at col-lege. Then for another six months I did telephone counselling under supervision at night from 10 p.m. to 8 a.m. When I was counselling the people who phoned, I felt the incredible suffer-ing they were going through. I realized the difficulties some people have and that some situations are shocking.

Until then I had been mainly in contact with Buddhist laypeople. I wanted to go out into the world like the Buddha and talk to whoever I came in contact with. I felt that to stay in a temple and talk only to the laypeople who wanted to hear about the Buddhadharma would be like a frog who thinks that the world is equivalent to the bottom of a well.

It has been worthwhile, but I have felt a lot of suffering. I have cried a lot. Why do I cry? Sometimes I wonder why can't all sentient beings live together peacefully and without suffer-ing? Why can't people live from the love which is in their beau-tiful minds? Why are there so many people living in such pain and experiencing problems in their lives? While praying in front of the Buddha, I ponder these questions and I cry.

The role of the counsellor is not to apply a ready-made solution, but to see everything from the other person's point of view. We must become like a dear friend to that person, someone who understands and accepts that person totally. We must become so intimate we abandon all screens. If we think on one side there is the client and on the other the counsellor or teacher, then this is not true counselling and it will not work.

I am also concerned about deaf people and wanted to communicate the Buddha's teaching to them. For three months I learned sign language and enjoyed discussions with deaf people in it, but because of my work at the radio station I had to stop.

## Helping Our Neighbour in Difficulty

Every Friday on the radio, there is 'Helping our Neighbour in Difficulty' hour. Volunteers find people in difficulty, research their situation and during the programme give a report. We hear the voice of the person in difficulty as they tell us about their circumstances and what is needed. Then on the air we get phone calls from people who can help them. Money is sent and once a week I distribute it. During the last 18 months 70 families have been helped. Meeting the families in difficulty, I feel like an envoy of the Bodhisattvas.

One of my strongest memories is of an old woman. During the Korean War she had to come over to the South with her young son, but her husband and elder son were cut off in the North and had to stay there. She raised her son and he studied hard at university. Just before graduation he had an accidental fall, his mind became strange and he had to be taken to psychiatric hospital.

Now the son is 55 and has been in hospital for the last 30 years. To visit him the mother has to have about £20 for the bus fare and some treats, but because recently she did not even have that, she could not go. She was very sad and cried every day.

On top of it she had a pain in her left leg and could not walk properly. She is a Buddhist and prayed at home every day, because she could not go to a temple.

Through the 'Helping Hour' we went to visit her and offered help. Some taxi drivers offered to drive her free of charge, enabling her to visit her son from time to time. Because he is visited more often by his mother, he has improved and is much better.

After this old woman was helped by the programme, she said to me: 'In this world nothing comes about without a reason.' It is important to remember this, particularly for people who look down on others or who do not help people who are poor and suffering. What I have, I want to share with people in need, who have more difficulty than me.

When she was given a bowl of rice or some goodies, this old lady would share it with other old ladies of her neighbourhood. When we gave her some money, she did not keep it just for herself, but shared it with other people too. Every day she gets up at 3 a.m., prays to the Buddha and meditates. When I meet people like her, I feel so much joy and that my work is worthwhile. I am happy that we both have karma with the Buddha that enabled us to meet each other.

## The Lotus Village

Another story which struck me deeply is that of a man who is very disabled. He is 37 now and had poliomelitis when he was three. Since then he has no use of his lower body and can only move about in a little cart. Both his parents died, leaving him and his three siblings alone. The sibling born after him was also disabled and died. The other two brothers left home and he has never heard from them since.

For years he lived in a little tiny cubbyhole with just space enough to sit and sold newspapers. He would save the money he earned until he had accumulated a certain sum. Then he would call a taxi and, having to pay double fare because of his disability, would go to his mother's grave to pay his respects, offer some food and pray. In front of his little hut, there was a bakery taken care of by a young couple who were Buddhists. For eight years they helped him by giving him food.

One day a big road was planned, his hut was going to be destroyed and he had nowhere to go. We were told about him and after a radio appeal we received £800. We tried to find a new place for him through social services and disabled services, but no place would receive him because he had no regular income and was so handicapped.

However, in the northeast province there is a place called the Lotus Village, created by a Buddhist monk who helps everyone – disabled, homeless and mentally troubled people. The monk is father and mother to them all. Finally a phone call came from this monk telling us to bring him there and that he would care for him. During the harvest festival, when Koreans go to their ancestors' graves, the monk takes him from Yechon to Inchon [a long way] to pray at his mother's grave and then brings him back.

## The Light in the Dark

In the morning I get up at dawn and before chanting in front of the Buddha, I practise breathing evenly for 20 minutes. Then I reflect on how to speak sincerely and truthfully by meditating on the meaning of the chants. Before leaving I read a chapter from a Buddhist sutra, as I want to transmit and express the ideas and words of the Buddha more than my own ideas and words.

At 7 a.m. I go to the radio station. My days are busy and sometimes I come back late at 8 or 9 p.m. Even though I might be very tired, every evening I chant and pay my respects to the

Buddha, my teacher. Then I reflect on how I spent the day and meditate, counting the breath for 20 minutes before falling asleep. I compose the breath in the morning and in the evening as a way to bridge my whole day with spiritual practice.

In this world amidst suffering we can see happiness in the same way as in the dark we can see light. Inside such great suffering are many people who are ready to share their happiness. Reflecting on the money we receive, I see many people who send money regardless of their circumstances, without discriminating between themselves and others.

For me it is more than money; I see these donations as the sincerity and good heart of the people. For someone without a house, we try to find a house; for people who need surgery, we make it possible for them to have an operation; for orphans, we give them school expenses and try to fulfil the role of parents. We try to help people in need. If the Buddha were alive today he would do this too.

# 15
## your eyes are precious gems
## Sister Chan Khong

Sister Chan Khong is a Vietnamese Buddhist nun dedicated to
social change. For more than three decades she has worked
closely with Thich Nhat Hanh in Vietnam and at his
community-in-exile in France, Plum Village. She is always
looking for ways to resolve difficulties and celebrate the joys of
a life of service. Plum Village often resounds with her exquisite
singing and is enriched by her calm presence.

## Stopping and Looking Deeply

At home I suggest you spend at least five minutes in the morning just stopping. Buddhist meditation is divided into two parts: stopping and looking deeply. Stopping is samatha and looking deeply is vipassana.

Only five minutes are needed for those who are very busy and feel they have no time for sitting meditation. You can practise at least five minutes before going to work: follow your breath, mentally reciting, 'Breathing in, I calm the body and mind; breathing out, I smile.' Or you can focus on this image offered by Thay [Thich Nhat Hanh]: 'Breathing in, I see myself as a flower; breathing out I feel fresh.' In the evening, at dinner you could take the time to stop and follow three breaths before eating.

The second part of Buddhist meditation is looking deeply. If you are conscious throughout the day, you will not fall into the trap of unwholesome mental and physical activities. The evening is very important because you can become mindful of all the activities you have done during the day.

Even though you might try to act mindfully, it is easy to forget. In the evening you can reflect on your motivation. Maybe you have been invited to become president of some organization to save the boat people and you are excited about it. When you look deeply, you are surprised to see you do not care about the boat people as much as having an exalted position. So you have to look deeply in order to see your thoughts, motivations and intentions better. Then you will not be attracted by fame, money or reputation under the guise of being socially conscious.

## The Breath Is a Refuge

The Buddha practised conscious breathing until he died. After he became enlightened he practised mindfulness of breathing in order to live in worldly activities without being caught in them. Often we think that when one becomes a Buddha, it is permanent. But becoming a Buddha is also impermanent, so our Buddhahood has to be nurtured all the time. If we are too sure that we are enlightened, we can sink. People who practise must continue to practise all the time.

The Buddha explained that although our bodies are here, our minds might be far away. Our breath is the link that can unify body and mind. Any meditator who is just beginning has to learn the 16 ways of conscious breathing that the Buddha taught in the *Anapanasati Sutra*. My teacher, Thich Nhat Hanh, has summarized these 16 exercises in short poems like: 'In – out – deep – slow, calm – ease – smile – release, present moment – wonderful moment.'

That sounds so simple, as if for children, but even people who have practised 50 years have to use this all the time, especially when they are troubled, angry or cannot find peace. We are not always at peace, so we have to go back to our breath all the time – when we are on the train, in a plane, even in a big meeting, because we cannot always go to the meditation hall to practise.

Our breath is a great refuge. When we go back to our breath we can separate ourselves from disturbances. For example, in an argument during a meeting, we dissociate ourself from our mouth, from our ears. We breathe consciously four or five times in order to be sure our mind is present with the movement of the breath.

After that we can switch into calm, ease, calm, ease. Or we can notice that our breath is deeper or slower. Then we feel calm. This is because the air calms every cell of our lungs until it goes even deeper, follows the blood everywhere and calms every cell in our body. Breathe in and ease. Ease all the nerves, making the cells calm. Smile and breathe the air out, release all your worries; so calm, ease, smile and release.

When we smile, we release all the tension in our muscles. We not only smile with our faces, we also smile with every cell in our bodies. We leave every cell smiling, smiling and releasing. When we feel peaceful and calm, we can come back to the present moment. We can be a Buddha only in the present moment; from being a monster we can transform ourselves into a Buddha.

There is no difference between inner and outer. When you go out and feel angry, go back to your breath: in, out, calm, ease, smile, release. When you feel that the anger is too big, that with many people around you cannot solve it, you can even go to the toilet or restroom to do walking meditation. First stop and calm yourself, and then look deeply in order to see the problem, to work out how you can overcome the problems and transform the negative situation into a better one.

Looking deeply is not intellectual thinking or speculation. It means trying to be in the skin of the other person in that situation. You try to feel the difficulties from the other person's viewpoint. On that basis you can understand and accept the other person. If you need to discuss something or make the other person understand, you can do so from that basis. Every aspect of your work will become more acceptable to the other person after you have been in their skin.

## Encountering Life with Joy and Peace

What brings me the most joy in my spiritual life is seeing other people happy. I like contributing something to others' happiness. The seed is very strong in me to be happy with other people. I want to carry everyone to the other shore.

I try to be as mindful as possible when I walk, when I sit, when I eat. I do not aim for any particular results. All the good seeds of my intention are there. When I am still and clear, all the good seeds in my store of consciousness, such as openness and the willingness to help, will come up by themselves.

My aim is to arrive at joy, peace and stillness, deeply encountering life and renewing life in every second. When I am with someone, I try to be as available as possible, fresh and smiling. When I go to the post office to get some stamps, I try to smile and be as kind and mindful as I can to the postmaster. In every step I have no other aim than to make each step mindful, and when I do so, my great wish to bring happiness to people comes up by itself.

I do my best to practise aimlessness. When I practise aimlessness, people may think I do not do anything, just dwell in peace and joy, but I am very active and have many responsibilities. If I think too much about this, I could become confused. But if I practise aimlessness, joy and peace in every step, trying to be fresh and smiling, renewing myself every second, then when I meet someone, I can be with them fully.

When I was a student I loved working with poor people in the slums of Saigon. My school was organized so that there were not many tests during the year, but at the end of the year I needed to know 3,000 pages of biology and parasitology practically by heart. During the whole year I spent my time with the poor in slum areas and I had only two months before the exam. I told myself at that point that I had to study seriously for the exams or my father would be sad. For two months I studied 60–100 pages every day. I enjoyed doing this and I went over each page again and again systematically. In two months I got through all 3,000 pages. It is a matter of organizing, but after organizing you can practise aimlessness.

## Social Justice on Earth

Social work has always been part of my life. At first I did not know anything about the dharma, although I was born into a generous family who liked to help poor people. When I was young I wanted to learn something that would enable me to help poor people on a large scale. I decided on academic study. I thought I could use Western knowledge to improve social justice, so I was attracted to Marxism. Then I recognized that many of my fellow countrymen, who were Marxists, were causing a lot of suffering. I saw that Marxism was not the way to really help people, but I did not know which way to turn. Slowly I started to study Buddhism and I was impressed by the teachings of the Buddha.

I wanted to use those teachings to create social justice, but the Buddhist monks I met at that time did not agree with me. They said that I needed to be enlightened first. Only when I became enlightened could I help people. Many monks were so conservative that they believed being a woman was an obstacle and they told me that I needed to practise in order to be reborn as a man. Then after many lifetimes I might become a Buddha.

I thought I did not need to become a man, I did not need to become a Buddha, I just needed to use some of the teachings of the Buddha to bring social justice on Earth. After looking around for many years, I met Thich Nhat Hanh. Thay said that you only need to do one action and if you do it mindfully, you will become enlightened. He told me the story of a monk who only practised sewing, but sewing mindfully, coming back with each breath, being totally in the action; after six years, he was enlightened. Similarly, there was a teacher who only pounded rice and another who became enlightened while cooking.

I decided I could become enlightened by being a social worker. I did not need to become a man and go through many lives to become a Buddha. I could help poor people and by alleviating their suffering, slowly they would become part of my path.

## 'I Have Not Said a Word'

People give me various titles – 'social worker', 'nun', 'practitioner' – but these are just words. A social worker must be a good practitioner of mindfulness. If a social worker works mindfully, with deep understanding, her work will be wonderful, like an artist's work. Words are only temporary and contingent labels. I am just as I am.

After teaching for 45 years, the Buddha said: 'I have not said a word.' He meant that he had to use words to help carry people from this shore of misery to the shore of understanding, but after we are transported to the other shore, we should not cling dogmatically to the raft, i.e. the words or teachings.

When I first came into contact with Buddhism in the 1950s, I wanted to become a nun, someone who abandoned everything – job, fame, glory, etc. – in order to live entirely for other people with great heart and understanding. The word 'nun' seemed so beautiful to me. But then I met nuns who did not fit the image I had idealized, so I decided to become a nun without form. It meant I did not shave my head for many years, but only practised as a nun. Recently, in 1988, I decided to become a nun, and was ordained by Thich Nhat Hanh at Vulture Peak in India.

I decided to become a nun because after 30 years of war and 17 years of Communism in Vietnam, our people's suspicion is so great that they daren't trust anyone except monks and nuns. They have suffered so much and they need to talk to someone about their personal difficulties. So I decided to become a nun to make it easier for refugees and those still in the country to trust me.

## Your Eyes Are Precious Gems

I always try to help Vietnamese families who are in conflict. Sometimes the father hates the mother and vice versa. The children suffer, or quarrel with their father because they do not respect each other. I try to help these families resolve their conflicts so they can live in harmony.

Working as a dharma teacher I have transformed many families, many of whom later want to help me in my work and even become social workers themselves. Some have set up their own committees in Europe, Australia and America to help hungry children in Vietnam. So now I do not have to devote all my time to helping hungry children directly, but instead I work with those I can transform who, in turn, help me in my work for social change.

With many families, I have to pretend to teach the children the dharma in order to reach the grown-ups as well. As I speak to their children the mother and father are deeply moved, and they can be transformed too.

I like to teach the dharma without using big words, especially with children. I might say: 'Today I have a gift for all of you. It is not medicine, it is not food. Do you know that your eyes are precious gems? When you open them, you see your mummy, your daddy and the blue sky. You can see all kinds of forms, all kinds of colours. Have you visited the school for the blind nearby? They do not see and you have these precious jewels.

'You have an even more precious gift. Look at your mummy. She is so sweet and she looks after you so hard. Please appreciate how precious it is that she is there, because one day it might be too late. Be aware.'

In this way I tell them to be in touch with the preciousness of each other.

## Listening

The first family I took care of, the daughter complained that her father was a nasty man. At 3 a.m., every morning, he woke up and played the sitar. No one could sleep. His playing would disturb the whole family. I went to their house and during a meal I listened to the father and the children express their complaints.

I realized that when the father woke at 3 a.m. to play the sitar, he was homesick. For him, playing the sitar was touching his homeland, the deep cultural background of Vietnam which the daughter, who grew up in the West, did not understand. For him, the sitar was not music, but his homeland – a sister who was sick without food, a brother who was in jail, many things he could not express in any other way.

His daughter spoke English and had grown up like an ordinary Australian girl. She knew nothing about Vietnam and it was driving him mad. He did not know how to explain it to her, so he played the sitar. He even broke some objects to express his anger. When I mentioned this to Thay, he suggested they spend more time together, being less busy in order to speak and listen to each other, to share their suffering.

I organized for them to help people who are suffering in Vietnam and this helped the whole family. At first, because the daughter in the West was not in touch with the suffering in Vietnam, she did not really care. But they started to help a number of people among their relatives and the whole family began to listen to the father.

Then I explained to the father: 'Your daughter is tired, she works in an office. When she comes home she is exhausted, she needs to relax. Can you help her to do that?' In this way the family learned to listen to and respect each other.

## Festivals and Celebrations

I use singing and music as part of the practice. Music is art and it can touch people deeply. People often remind me that a nun is not supposed to sing, but in every Buddhist temple there is chanting. Chanting is spiritual music. A song which expresses spirituality can water the spiritual seed in people. I do not discriminate between music and chanting. It is enough that it is beautiful and deep, and touches the heart of people. Practising singing meditation means that you sing with all your heart and mind. I sing with my eyes, my voice, my whole being.

We have many festivals at Plum Village which celebrate life. One is called a tangerine festival. When 20 children are in a group, eating 20 tangerines, looking deeply into the tangerines, enjoying peeling, smelling the skin and tasting the juice, that is a real celebration. It is quite different from eating a tangerine in forgetfulness. We have various festivals like that.

In some festivals, we renew contact with our roots and people come to appreciate and feel their culture better. We have a commemoration of boat-people day, for example. All the Vietnamese children know about their parents having escaped by becoming boat people. Because of their past poverty and desperation the parents always remind the children not to waste even a single grain of rice. But they often repeat the stories so often that the children just become bored with them.

I invite the children who are the least interested to be actors in their parents' stories. After acting out these events they really feel in touch and experience what it was to be a boat person. I choose a real letter from some little girl who has escaped from Vietnam on a boat and I ask these children to read it in front of a big audience. Because the atmosphere is so solemn, the readers are moved themselves and everyone else is moved also.

After that they know who they are, why their parents behave the way they do and why their parents do not like war. It is our aim to help people to feel for their traditional values, their deepest roots. A festival is a beautiful way to do this joyfully, in celebration. It helps people get in touch more easily.

## True Emptiness

My ordination name, Chan Kong, means 'True Emptiness'. In Buddhism the word 'emptiness' is a translation of the Sanskrit *sunyata* which means 'empty of a separate self'. This is not a negative or despairing term. It is a celebration of interconnectedness, of interbeing. It means that nothing can exist by itself alone, that everything is inextricably interconnected with everything else.

I know that I must always work to remember that I am empty of a separate self and full of the wonders of this universe, including the generosity of my grandparents and parents, and the many friends and teachers who have helped and supported me along the path. We 'inter-are' and therefore we are empty of an identity that is separate from our interconnectedness.

# 16
## who is healing?
### Daehaeng Sunim

Daehaeng Sunim is a Korean nun who is a famous healer. She was born in 1926 and suffered great difficulties in her early life under the Japanese occupation of her country. She was ordained in her twenties and spent many years deep in the mountains living frugally and practising meditation. During this time she developed healing power.

The nuns in her centre are very earnest and conversation turns immediately to meditation in everyday life, their aim being to watch their minds throughout the day and trust in the One Mind. They do not practise much sitting meditation as they think they must move with the times and not make a distinction between busyness and stillness.

The abbess, a disciple of Daehaeng Sunim, is small but quite fierce. She receives the people who come from all over Korea to be healed by Daehaeng Sunim and asks their reasons for coming – a bad back, a painful stomach, mental problems, troubles with husband or son (for it is mainly women who come). As soon as they speak about their ailments, the abbess tells them this is not a hospital, this is a place of practice. Why do they want to see Daehaeng Sunim? Only they can cure their own disease. All will see the healing nun finally, but only after pondering more deeply about their motivation and the source of their disease.

When someone comes to visit me, whatever suffering or diffi-culties they might have, mental or physical, I tell them to gather all their abilities together and then leave everything entirely to the *Ju In Gong* [master of the body]. The *Ju In Gong* is the self that enables the present 'I' to move, speak, eat and think. The source of the universe is directly connected to that of the mind, therefore the source is called *Ju In Gong*.

To watch the mind in everything means that in everyday life there is nothing that is not meditation. It also means that when inquiring into a koan there is nothing that is not the koan. We cannot say we are holding the koan separately somewhere else. There is no separation when it comes down to discovering our true self, as the original truth of the universe is undivided.

You must believe in and know yourself. In order to know whatever suffering and difficulty you might have, you must leave it to the inner master inside yourself. There is no need to attach yourself to your suffering, because all things are empty and there is no place where you can attach yourself. For this reason, let go of it and then, just as it is, it will disappear.

According to how you have lived in the past, all things are naturally recorded in your destiny. As something is recorded, so it will appear in the present time. Put everything down and leave it at the place where it has occurred. If you do this, both good and bad karmas will melt and disappear. The tape recorder which has kept records of all karmas will become empty. What should be recorded onto an empty tape? You decide.

Lay down everything, all you know or don't know. If you know something, you will also not know something and then you cannot know the principle of non-duality. Whatever it is, all you may know, let go of it. If you do not let go, I cannot meet with your true self.

## Everyday Life is Meditation

I live as a nun, leaving everything aside, and in this way I act without making any difference. Let's live without making any difference. When you do something, can you say that you have truly done anything? Looking, hearing, talking – everything comes out of an infinite variety of things moment by moment.

When you see something, hear something or do something, can you say you have seen, heard or done anything? The world of the spirit is all-encompassing and you could call this the One Mind of the spirit. It is like space – you cannot see it or grasp it, but still the mind exists.

Quietness alone is not meditation. Lots of noise is not meditation either. What is called 'meditation' is also not stuck on the word 'koan'. Standing meditation, lying meditation and sitting meditation – all these are meditations. In all life there is nothing that is not meditation. Whatever I do – going to the toilet, eating, sleeping – all is meditation. Where could you stick a word of any kind? Even what is called 'meditation', that word too you cannot hold on to, because it is as it is.

I teach the same to monks, nuns or laypeople. Because there is nothing in life that is not meditation, everyday life is meditation. Just as it is, watching, just as it is, doing, this is meditation. For this reason every person cures their own illness. They make their own suffering and difficulties disappear, they keep their family harmonious, and in this way they make progress. I cannot give them compassion and wisdom; they can only obtain and know these by themselves. If you watch, if you experiment, wisdom grows and problems are solved.

People have problems according to the workings of karma. You must reflect on yourself and not harbour any resentment, acting and speaking softly. All things you leave to the *Ju In Gong*. If you do everything softly, everything can be solved. When it is dark, if you light a lamp you can live brightly.

## Nothing Is Fixed

Keeping the precepts means that you place everything inside yourself. Do not blame anyone else. If you live without greed, then not only will you keep the 100, 200, 300 rules, but also you will be able to watch everything totally. Wisdom is included in this. Where else could it be? It is not apart from this.

Emptiness means that what you see is not fixed. You can see and hear this or that, go here or there, meet this or that person, eat this or that. Nothing is fixed. For this reason, when I do something, I cannot say I have done something, and when I see something, I cannot say I have seen something. Even I am empty. All is empty.

The Buddha means the origin of life. The teaching means that you see and do not see, everything in the world, all joins and revolves together. The interpenetration of things is the teaching. For this reason the Buddha's teaching has no barriers, frontiers or limitations; Buddhism is the expression of truth all over.

Westerners are inclined to think too much about their state of mind and suffer as a result. When suffering comes, if you leave it to the One Mind the mind becomes peaceful. Then you have no problems in your practice and no longer follow wandering thoughts. Outside you are not caught and inside becomes a practice of watching, guarding, experimenting.

## Healing

You yourself are the Medicine Buddha, Avalokitesvara Bodhisattva, Shakyamuni Buddha, all things. So you can rest in yourself, but you must also watch and guard your mind. In this way people are able to cure themselves while practising, then their suffering disappears.

My mind and the mind of a layperson are not two. It is similar to electricity: one needs two coils to make light. In the same way, the mind of the layperson and my mind combine together so that there is energy. Who can we say heals whom? Because the two minds resemble the thread and the lamp which need to touch each other and combine to make light, when there is contact, automatically light comes. For this reason neither side can say they did it. The only thing we can say is that the Buddha healed.

Is there anything which is not the Buddha? Inside the Buddha, there is the sentient being; inside the sentient being there is the Buddha. It reflects this way. Sometimes people ask me if the Way cures illnesses, but truthfully who is there to be cured of the illness? It is while somebody practises that they heal themselves.

# 17
## saying yes to love
## Maura Sills

Maura Sills, born in Scotland, is a Buddhist psychotherapist and co-founder of the Karuna Institute, situated on the wild and bracing heights of Dartmoor. Briefly a Buddhist nun, she is now married with a young daughter. She has great energy and gives herself deeply to her students and clients, combining professionalism with an elegant, light touch.

# A Spiritual Marriage

What is said about sex in Buddhism can be confusing. Meditation and living as a couple can help value the importance of separation in relationship. Sex is very important within a relationship. My sexual relationship with my husband and my own sexual nature have informed my meditation, and my meditation practice has deepened my sexual experience.

Most relationships end up in deep conditioning and dependency. Knowing this helps me realize that fundamentally a relationship is a paradox. I am totally alone and this liberates me within the relationship. I am not looking for security in my relationship; actually Franklyn and I got together because of our meditation. We married because we felt ready to marry and we knew it would be a spiritual marriage.

At times in my life I have chosen to be celibate, and I honour that choice and anybody who makes it. However, within some forms of Buddhism there is bad press about sex, the idea almost being that to be spiritual you must be non-sexual. My spirituality and my sexuality are so deeply connected that one is the door to the other. Sexual intercourse is part of lay and married life, and if spirituality and meditation cannot also be present, there is a basic mistake in the teachings. It is unhealthy if the teachings cannot inform sexual life and are only judgemental.

Some of my students project ideas about me because I practise Buddhism. One is that I must not have sex, another that I do not like it. Thus I become asexual in their eyes, which is strange because this is not how I experience myself at all. They have the idea that sex is at the lower end of human nature.

Most reports from Buddhists about sex come from celibate, non-married people. I am not only talking of physical sex, but of the inner relationship between male and female, which is essential and central. To ignore male energy, female energy or sexual energy in yourself, or in a relationship, is to ignore a whole illumination into the nature of life, into the nature of being a woman.

## Saying Yes to Love

I am not referring to sex without love. You cannot separate them once you go past a certain point. It is a wonderful joy to practise sexual love and it has a place in Buddhism. When I got married to Franklyn, as part of our wedding vows we chose the words from John Donne: 'I will choose to say yes to love as often as I can.' For me an adult relationship gives you that opportunity.

To choose to say yes to love is a practice and, like a meditation practice, sometimes it is very difficult. It is a vehicle to cultivate the opening of the heart with somebody who is also practising and hopefully who accepts the shortcomings of the other person. I do not mean colluding; I mean accepting. This can be an enormous encouragement and I believe people need encouragement to love.

This is one of the dilemmas of modern life that, for whatever reason, many children have not experienced adequate loving. They have experienced other things, but they have not really experienced total acceptance, total love. Most of our hearts have been hurt either by being open and betrayed or abused, or by being so closed off they could not feel love. Being in a continuing relationship where both of you are choosing as often as possible to say yes to love is an ongoing practice.

## The Way of the Warrior

There are enormous dangers in committed relationships and the biggest is fear of losing the relationship, whether it is with your partner or your children.

Recently I witnessed two pieces of therapeutic work, one

with a woman who lost her eight-month-old daughter four years ago. She could not bear this loss and had been in the hell realms for the last four years. It became apparent to me that this is the risk you take when you become a mother and I realize I am also attached to my daughter.

The other situation was a woman whose husband suddenly died within three hours a couple of years ago. She had totally died inside, and though functional and successful in her job, she was frozen. One woman was distraught and in the hell realms and the other looked like a hungry ghost, with nothing to take the place of the loss of her husband.

So for me, choosing love in a committed relationship, choosing love full stop, is the way of the warrior. It is the courageous way to live, to risk everything. I feel love and death are close together.

## Psychotherapy and Meditation

Meditation helps us to risk opening our heart to bring in love and kindness. It is essential to cultivate our ability to love, which feels almost artificial unless it is put to the test. Meditation can also enable us to survive the distress and pain of feeling mortal love. It can help in experiencing the cost of not-loving, but also in loosening our grip when we are attached and dependent in love.

Meditation connects us with the universal qualities of love, totally non-dependent on a personal connection, perhaps the sense of something that will not change. It is not just understanding the larger context, but experiencing support from the universal nature of life. This can be called faith.

There is a strong connection between therapy and meditation. Psychotherapy often says things similar to the early teachings of the Buddha: his search for truth, his inner inquiry, what he designated important. The journey, the inquiry in therapy, is very compatible with the journey and inquiry a meditator would make.

The power of psychotherapy is very similar to the power of meditation, which is the cultivation of awareness. A psychotherapy which is not involved with the study of consciousness, or does not have awareness practice as central to being human, cannot meet human needs today. Psychotherapy does not only concentrate on the cognitive mind, it also has the potential for a deeper, inner response or healing. The subliminal mind, the wise mind uncovered in our attentive awareness, is the mind we need to be reconnected with.

In Buddhism experience is not seen as a problem; it is how we respond, react and relate to an experience which is problematic. In transpersonal psychotherapy we see no matter how pathological or difficult the symptoms, they are trying to give us some information, to teach us something; they are the doorway to the subliminal mind, the wise mind.

There are differences between Buddhism and psychotherapy too. Within traditional Buddhist practice there is very little attention given to the personal, the self. Westerners who have a healthy sense of self can use meditation as their only tool, but there are many Westerners who have not even separated from their mothers. They have not gone through the maturation process that maybe most Easterners would have automatically negotiated. Because of a different sense of the individual and of the group, psychotherapy can help in working with the personality, the unresolved, maturational, individuational issues which must be dealt with in order to have a successful practice of meditation.

Sometimes Buddhism and psychotherapy are considered to be in opposition. This is a misperception. A meditation practice that embraces the personality and a psychotherapeutic practice that embraces an understanding of the nature of consciousness are both skilful models and can work in harmony. I see a movement of meditation practitioners starting to embrace psychotherapy and of psychotherapists being open to exploring the nature of consciousness.

Meditation has brought to my psychology a sense of the mystery of being human. It has helped me trust the unknown in psychotherapy and has allowed me to develop more patience, tolerance, acceptance and awareness of the multiple layers of resistance. It has enabled me to see the psychological layers the person is struggling with and where they are free. It has helped me to help the person.

## Relaxing the Tension

In 1971 I was attracted to Chinese medicine and tai-chi, and my teacher was as much Taoist as Buddhist. Gradually I realized we were meditating. We were doing mostly inner energy practices, using the breath to circulate energy [chi] and very slow-moving chi kung exercises to develop an awareness of the chi. At other times we were told to sit silently and just watch the mind.

I studied Chan Buddhism for about eight years, then in 1978 went to America, where I started to practise psychotherapy.

Franklyn was a student of Rina Sircar and I also felt inspired by her. When her teacher, Taungpulu Sayadaw, came to America, I decided it would be a great opportunity to take temporary ordination and practise with him.

He taught simple insight meditation, a mindfulness practice with special attention given to different personality attributes. I watched many sensations, many feelings and spent a lot of time looking at the body, which I found very helpful. However, neither psychotherapy nor meditation had altered the tension in my body, though through these practices this anxiety was kept tolerable.

One of my teachers recommended the Nyingma Institute in Berkeley and their technique, *Kum Nye*, which was described as relaxation. I thought a Buddhist form of meditative relaxation could help me lose this anxiety. However, I realized after the first few days of the practice that it was not about making me feel better. It was about working with all the resistances and failings of the personality. I did a three-month intensive practice which at the time was very hard for me. It was only when I left the institute years later that I realized how important that practice was.

Now I both teach and practise *Kum Nye*, but I would not say that it is my main meditation practice. I feel it is more a maintenance practice for the body-mind and energies, and in some ways it is similar to the earlier practices of the Taoist/Chan tradition. My personal practice is insight. I just continue to practise sustained attention, watching to see if I can keep my mind sharp for the impact of perceptions.

## Two-Person Practice

For a long time I thought sitting silently on a cushion on retreat or during the day was meditation, but over the years my practice has evolved and I have become more active in my daily life and in my work as a psychotherapist, trainer and teacher. Now my meditation is to be with another person in relationship.

Sustained attention is still vital and this has been my main learning vehicle. Although I have moved to a two-person joint practice, I still need to sit and withdraw from relationship. The change is to see the value in both instead of only seeing the sitting practice as important.

It can be similar in psychotherapy. You see a client once or twice a week, but the mistake can be for both client and therapist to think this is the important time. In the same way for me as a meditator the mistake was to think that sitting was the important thing. Both views have shifted and I realize it is how I am outside of these times that is significant. If I have not changed in these non-practice situations then the psychotherapy and the meditation are simply avoidances.

My two-person practice is in the context of a special relationship, but not with a special person. Two people enter a special relationship which requires joint presence and awareness practice.

I learn from relationships in general, but not in the same way as I have learned and continue to learn from being with students, clients and groups.

## Beginners

I would recommend an easy meditation practice in the beginning, giving people something to do with sensations. The ability to feel sensations is available to most people and it gives them a sense of doing something which can help transformation, or develop insight or clarity, whatever the intention of the practice is.

*Kum Nye* is a good beginner's practice, if it is taught gently. It helps concentrate the mind and reduce the amount of avoidance that quite often resurrects itself much later in the practice. You work with the personality and conditioning right from the beginning.

In psychotherapy, we start with the breath. For me, meditation and psychotherapy have the similar starting-point of following the breath into the body and becoming aware of sensations and movements so that the attention is pulled towards the physical. When we manage to become more present with our physical body then a sense of ease can occur.

## Everyday Life

In everyday life I would recommend mindfulness, sustained attention and a basic slowing down. Discipline and intention are important. I do not mean an external discipline, but taking a certain decision about how to be in daily life. To work within these limitations and intentions feels very useful. Meditation, activities, relationships, working with what we have and what there is, this is all we need.

How I practise in everyday life fluctuates enormously. Generally I do some short physical exercises followed by meditation. I like to withdraw and disengage first thing in the morning and just be quiet, usually doing *Kum Nye* practices in order to withdraw attention from activities and come back more into myself. I am very responsive and if this does not happen for some reason I am too much in my actions and too responsive to daily activities.

As I work with people most of the time, this is where my practice has to begin, as soon as I walk through the door. So when I am with people, I see this as a good opportunity to practise mindfulness of response, action and mind-states. The sense of being in relationship with a person informs not just myself and the other person, but also the relationship, which is not independent from us.

## Loosening Up

Some students entering the Karuna psychotherapy training are from a Buddhist tradition and were introduced to meditation before they explored their personality and sense of self. Their meditation has been built upon a quite faulty or damaged ego-structure and this surfaces with practice.

Often vipassana practitioners have too much control. Their awareness has reduced the potential of experiences arising so they are only able to be with a limited range of arising experiences. Dryness can occur through control and if it does there is a need to loosen up. The naming in some forms of vipassana can also give a false sense of control, so a practice to loosen these people up is useful. Some of the transformative *Kum Nye* practices offer a vehicle for loosening up the ego through the body taking back more control.

Certain aspects of meditation are more useful than others for Westerners. Practices which balance concentration with sustained attention and at the same time work with love or the energy of the heart are very enriching. Practices which allow compassion to arise, based on seeing the nature of suffering in other people, can also be beneficial.

Sometimes Westerners have a false sense of worth. Somehow the values of competition and achievement in Western society have extinguished an inner sense of truth, authenticity and realness. These people need a practice which opens up not only the experience of their own meditation and arising experience but also helps them to see others' experience as important.

The meditation practice of first loving yourself and then others is almost impossible for Westerners. If you can truly see suffering in another, then there is an opportunity to relate this back to yourself. Often we are more able to see and feel compassion and *metta* for other people first, and only then see that what we are actually looking at is ourselves as well. We need to see meditation as interdependent and interconnected. It is the study and nature of consciousness, so it takes us beyond the person and we do not remain quite so egocentric.

## Meditation in Relationship

In daily life you have to practise fast meditation. You have to practise meditation in relationship. Whether it is relationship with what you do, with people or with experiences, you have to be a very fast meditator. It is like fast walking practice and slow walking practice, and you must value the laylife as potentially as enlightening as the monastic one.

Obviously there are problems in laylife because of material possessions, children and partners; we become involved a lot more and there are more positions we have to negotiate. However, it can be positive because you can watch yourself moving between positions. You can get soft, though, because soft options are there. You can be distracted and become distant from your inner life. You can avoid fear in your life because you can take drugs, food, drink or whatever. You can feed away the fear.

Conversely, in monastic life your role is pretty fixed and you work with reduced positions, but there are difficulties too. There is a lack of flexibility in catering for individual needs, though there is too much catering for these needs in laylife perhaps. On the emotional level there is less acceptance of, and fewer outlets for, emotional distress or expressions of distress. In a monastic situation you are not informed by the state of the world, so your views of it might become a little rigid.

## Teacher?

There are people I feel I can learn from who have been in practice longer than myself and who are wiser, but I do not have a particular teacher now. The teacher I was ordained by was the Venerable Taungpulu Sayadaw. When I met him he was in his late eighties. He was a forest monk from Burma who had spent 13 years in solitary retreats. He did not speak English so all my instructions came through an interpreter.

Till then I never thought I wanted a teacher like Sayadaw, because of my feminist views and because there were so many people devoted to him. Before he came to California I felt some negativity towards him. It was a great surprise when we met him at the airport because I had a completely unthought response and bowed down to him, not knowing how I got down there. It just felt as if I had been put there. It was the only time in my life that I found and was found by a teacher. It was totally non-verbal and though the translated teachings were excellent, I did not feel they were the teaching. In some way

Sayadaw picked me up and his presence was the biggest teaching I ever experienced.

Nowadays my main inspiration comes from people, often from despairing of people and then watching a miracle take place. Time and again I run out of expertise and almost give up, then something changes for someone or a miracle happens in a relationship. When I think I have reached the bottom of my ability to trust, it is enriching. Through sustained attention and deep listening miracles can happen and that is what keeps me going.

## Ethics

If you come back to being a true human being, resensitizing yourself, then morality arises spontaneously. I have seen this in practice time and again. Many people have lost their inner sense of ethics, the inner self-regulating morality based upon natural responsiveness to the nature of the universe. People in the West have lost the inner sense of what they need to eat, how they need to sleep, how much to express; they have lost the whole biorhythm because of Western culture.

Because we have lost our way with ethics we are like cripples, leaning against other ethical systems and codes. Buddhism has a good ethical system and it is useful, but usually we take it on as an external ruler or use it as a crutch before we develop our inner morality and inner self-regulation. I think Westerners tend to take it on and then hit themselves over the head or measure their achievements by it. It is the male principle gone totally wrong.

## The Human Condition

The wisdom of Buddhism must become more available to ordinary non-Buddhist people. Dharma is not a Buddhist possession and we can use some skilful practices from Buddhism to

respond to circumstances in the world today. The older historical experiences of Buddhism should not be diluted, but they
must be retranslated into ways that all people can get into.

Buddhism has become enshrouded in dogma, structures and
forms. Forms can be helpful in some way, but in the world
today, Buddha-mind has to inform as directly as possible without cultural screens. The human beingness must be brought
back into Buddhism. Some forms of Buddhism seem to have
lost their trust in the human condition, but this is how we are,
who we are and it is what we have to work with. It is not a mistake and we are not disadvantaged by it; the human condition
is real even if total reactive ignorance is where we get the information from.

The path of the psychotherapist and the meditator is sensi-
tivity to being human. If we are resensitized to the human condition then dharma and Buddhism will become flowing truth,
not something learned and separate. It is as if we disrespect the
human condition and see it as something to be transformed,
transcended or let go of. I am not just talking about the ego, I
am talking about the whole human condition. This is where the
whole information is, embodied here in human beings, and we
must re-empower the individual.

# 18
## the dharma of family life
### Christina Feldman

Christina Feldman is a meditation teacher and mother of two
children living in Totnes, Devon. She is active at Gaia House, a
meditation retreat centre she co-founded in 1984, and totally
dedicated to her children. Amidst all this busyness she is
unflappable, ordinary and charming. She is the author of *Quest
of the Warrior Woman* (Aquarian, 1994) and other books.

# A Challenging Situation

I was determined to continue practising when I had a family. So many people had told me that I would never be able to do it. If I had children I was supposed to stop teaching because they would consume all my time and attention; meditation and teaching were things I would take up again later. I was determined to disprove these opinions and stereotypes, though this was not my only motivation.

It was a challenge because there were so few teachers who were parents and even fewer women teachers with children. So when I had my first child, people expected me to stop teaching, and when expecting my second, they said, 'Now *surely* she will stop teaching!'; but I did not. Having children did not mean the conclusion of being a meditator and a teacher, entering exclusively into parenthood, and I felt this would be in many ways an even greater challenge to the practice.

It is easy to meditate when you live in a monastery. In the same way it is easy to be a meditator in an ideal, protected environment like a retreat. But the acid test of the dharma is our capacity to live it and apply it, not only when it is pleasant and easy, but also in challenging situations. I had a strong inward determination to continue my practice and my teaching.

I am fortunate in being a meditation teacher because I have never had to have a nine to five routine. I have also had the support of my partner, who has a deep respect for the dharma and the teaching of it. He was very willing to support me and help care for the children. When the children were very young and much more demanding it took an extraordinary amount of discipline on my part to sustain a lively, exploring and ongoing practice and teaching.

When my children were babies I would often not start work or have time for silence, reflection or writing till nine or ten at night, and then only for a couple of hours. Parents know that in a couple of hours a baby is going to wake up. It took an enormous amount of discipline when the children were small and needy, and this was absolutely essential; my practice could never have continued without it.

Sometimes it was teeth-gritting to maintain the discipline; when the children were asleep it was much more attractive to read a book or lie down and relax. Yet still every night I took the time to meditate and by the end I was aware of having contributed to keeping alive an inner sense of direction, an inner sense of vision that was not defined by any of the other roles in my life. Every time I began, it brought a sense of freshness and direction into the next day. Every single one of those times was worth it, even if sometimes I was in a kind of stupor.

## Meditation and Parenting

As my children grew up, they gave a sense of immediacy to my practice. Parenting challenges you at every level of your being. All the things that are important in meditation practice – patience, forgiveness, letting go, compassion, steadfastness and equanimity – are the things that are also important in parenting. Children provide opportunities to develop, nurture and nourish these qualities in direct and dynamic ways.

Some of the things in meditation which bring greater depth, understanding and calmness, also work when you are with children. I find letting go is perhaps the most important connection between meditation and parenting – just not carrying images, images of what happened in the last moment, of what went wrong in the last moment into the next one. Living with this freshness and openness is what makes parenting a meditative experience rather than just a necessity.

If a parent were to go into a monastery for an intensive retreat, they would need equanimity, compassion, perseverance and discipline. If you invited a nun or monk into your house and asked them to look after your children, they would need to cultivate exactly the same qualities. It is essential to value these qualities as part of your life-journey, whatever the context. They are as important in intensive practice as in parenting.

I am very involved in my children's lives. I am closely connected to their education, have a good relationship with their teachers and help in their school fairly regularly. I try to offer my children useful extra-curricular activities and we spend a lot of their free time together, often in nature. We have a very open communication. As they grow older there will be areas in their lives they may not want me to be involved in. Already now, there are things they do not invite me to participate in and I am happy they do this.

The longest time they have been apart from me is eight days. I have always taken them with me when I teach retreats abroad. I have never wanted to be an absentee parent and my children are aware of their parents' availability. To me, being a conscious parent means being a willing participant in each other's lives. I feel the closeness we have now when they are young will create a firm foundation for their independence when they grow older.

Being a Buddhist parent means embodying a deep sense of ethics in the household, ethics which the children live by now, organically, in their own lives. It has to do with how we see the world, and a sense of interconnectedness and responsibility.

## Children's Spirituality

As my children grow older they are aware of how central the dharma is to my life. They are also very much included and I encourage them to have their own journey of reflection. They support me consciously in my work, my teaching and when they come with me on retreat.

Children seem to find their own ways of practising and my

role in life is not to mould my children into a particular form of dharma practitioner. Yet every parent inevitably influences their children through their actions, examples and words. It is important that my influence on my children is one which is skilful, wholesome and encourages them to question and understand.

I would recommend the ethical foundations of the dharma, the precepts, for children. They have been part of my children's lives since they could understand words and with this influence they have come to a deeper understanding of interconnectedness. They would not harm anything that is living, for example, as they understand from their own experience that this would be a violation of life. Obviously their ethics cannot be separated from their past influences and their parents, but they have integrated them. We teach our children about mindfulness, compassion and awareness through example. But you cannot *make* children be aware, you cannot force them to be a particular way. They have to travel their own journey and the parent is a guide, like a dharma teacher is a guide.

I have been teaching the family retreat at Barre [Massachusetts, America] for 10 years. The idea of the family retreat is to give parents an opportunity to practise without being separated from their children. We provide childcare and a few quiet hours in the day for parents to continue their meditation. This is unusual in the West, where very few meditation centres welcome children.

Usually parents have to separate themselves from their children to pursue or develop their own spiritual lives. From the children's point of view, this is a distorted approach, because spirituality is something their parents go away to do; their friends' parents go to church or synagogue, whilst their parents go away to meditate. Through the family retreats we began to look at ways of breaking down these disconnections.

Children have no idea what meditation is, so they regard spirituality as strange, foreign and out of context. It has become apparent to me that many children have no spiritual dimension in their lives. Their parents come from a generation which often renounced traditional religion and no longer went to church, so the children had no indigenous spiritual symbols in their lives. In America it is illegal to have religious education in schools; children are exposed to symbols of consumerism, pleasure and aversion instead. It is clear that Buddhism in the West needs to address this kind of division and contribute towards raising a new generation of spiritually aware people.

Spirituality can embrace everything in our lives, including parenting, relationships, interacting with other people and working. In this way it is not a disguise or a cloak we put on when we go into a retreat and take off when we leave. Including children in the retreat is a way of recognizing this. It has always been assumed in Western meditation teaching that a spiritual journey is adult territory and the spiritual lives of children are rarely addressed. It is as if children have no spiritual dimension and spiritual needs of their own. It seems we expect them to grow up in a Western culture, make whatever mistakes they need to make, collect whatever unresolved issues they need to collect and then come on a retreat when they are old enough to work it all out.

So with family retreats we started to include children for short periods and we would have a family meditation. The children would come to the meditation room once a day for half an hour and we would do some loving-kindness meditation and chant a little or perhaps do a ritual. I did not know how much the parents would accept my teaching the dharma to children, so in the first years it was minimal.

Over the years some of the children developed different needs, and new children came in. They wanted to have more places in the retreat which addressed their needs, rather than what other people thought they should have. As they grow up, they ask for more discussion groups, teaching and practice.

They do several periods of sitting and walking meditation. The younger children have a slightly different schedule, which is still changing.

Through working with the children, especially after they have been to the retreat more than once, I have found they have a certain willingness, openness and interest in learning the dharma which is really impressive.

Gradually I feel more confident in my capacity to teach the dharma to children and in their capacity to understand it. I think it is important and necessary to regard children as responsible spiritual beings. They may be immature physically and in their relationships, but they are blessed with a remarkable openness and capacity to learn.

## Liberation Has Little to Do with Excellence

Meditation is essentially about being awake in our lives and awake in ourselves. This is the heart of every path. Being attentive helps us to wake up, to be present, and the various practices and meditations are like clues that help us to be attentive. When I began to meditate I had no particular agenda of what I was looking for and I tended to rely on my teachers. They encouraged me to reflect upon compassion, or interconnectedness, or to see impermanence and emptiness within my experience.

What has evolved is a deep sense of faith and trust, both in the practice and the understanding that emerged from the practice. Now I find my meditation practice has a rhythm of its own, which often has little to do with my preferences. It often has its own, somewhat unpredictable momentum. There may be times when I specifically intend to develop concentration, loving-kindness or inquiry, but at other times the way my practice develops has nothing to do with conscious intention.

Concentration is not necessarily a prerequisite for insight, but calmness and tranquillity allow insight to penetrate more and be deeply transforming. Anyone who wants to awaken will benefit from learning how to develop calmness of being and clarity of mind, which are strongly related to developing attention.

There is a fine balance in conveying the benefits of attentiveness to people, yet not implying that the fulfilment of wakefulness rests upon personal excellence. The primary motivation for people beginning meditation is that they want to change and improve themselves, to find a way out of their personal pain and sorrow. Meditation is not just the pursuit of personal excellence and individual happiness; the spiritual path is concerned to end all suffering and its causes, and with developing boundless compassion and liberating insight.

The capacity to express wisdom through wise and compassionate action does not necessarily have anything to do with grand meditation experiences. The pursuit of perfection, of success through experiences, is one of the major neuroses of meditators, along with constant inner evaluation on the basis of presence or absence of experiences.

There are thousands of different meditation techniques, but the central theme in most is the intention of bringing the meditator closer to an experience of the present moment, thus the technique aims at developing attentiveness. Therefore the objects used – whether a mantra, the breath or the body – are not so important. They vary according to people's inclinations and to what is most useful for them. There is no hierarchy of meditation objects; using the breath as a way of developing attention is not better than using a mantra, or vice versa.

All beginners have everything they need to meditate. They do not need a lot of teaching to start meditation; everyone has a breath on which they can rest and focus their attention. You do not need a secret or mystical teaching, or a great deal of expertise or a special environment. This is the preciousness of meditation –

you do not need to be anyone special or anywhere special. Attentiveness is transforming and cuts through preoccupations, obsessions, projections and distortions, swiftly bringing inner calm and happiness.

## Attentiveness Brings Happiness

I try to keep my life uncluttered and make a point of not having a lot of chaos in my life. Chaos is not what I choose; it is not what I want and it does not enrich me. When I have a lot of work I give careful attention to how I approach each day. This is when I do things well. If I am connected with calmness, my life is calm even when I am busy. If I am not calm, I don't find calmness or harmony anywhere in my life. I do not feel confusion and chaos are intrinsic to living; they are more to do with the choices we make in our lives and our approach to living.

I love being attentive. Whether I am writing, speaking to people, being with meditators or reading, most of my life is spent paying attention. Sometimes we are tempted to think there is pleasure in distractedness, in being lost in fantasy or dreams, but in reality I feel this kind of disconnection from the present is painful.

It is important for me to create spaces to be alone, as I find solitude renewing and refreshing. In the West we have curious notions of relaxation. We read a book, listen to music, eat and daydream all at the same time and think we are taking care of ourselves. For me this is a recipe for chaos.

When I teach a retreat, I regard it very much as a retreat for myself. I do not think of it as a time for only teaching other people. It offers me a valuable opportunity to engage in more extended periods of quietness and meditation. Therefore I do not feel I am just a teacher.

I never have a sense of having arrived in my own practice; there always seems to be some level of unfolding, so my meditation feels vital and alive. If meditation were just something I did for other people it would be fairly dead in my life. It does not have that feeling and I hope it will never have a sense of arrival for me.

## Spiritual Community: A Desert or an Oasis?

To practise in everyday life it is important regularly to take time to be still and have contact with like-minded people. It is clear, though, that for many people a major gap exists between their daily lives and their retreat lives, and lacking a sense of spiritual community has a great deal to do with this. It is essential to emphasize the need for sangha. This is readily available in the East, where there are monasteries on almost every corner, but in the West there may be a long gap between spiritual connections and many people occupy a spiritual desert in their outer lives. If they are going through cycles of deepening on retreat and then losing it afterwards, they must look more radically at how they live, work and relate.

Many people place such emphasis on experiential insight that they devalue the path of reflective insight accessible outside of retreat. Experiential insight comes in intensive meditation, when there is a direct experience of emptiness, impermanence or the relationship between suffering and its causes. This is very direct and exposes us at a basic cellular level. But people find experiential insight is not liberating unless they apply it. What does it mean to let go in our lives, to live in a spirit of emptiness and compassion? This is reflective insight which is so much a part of the Tibetan tradition and has perhaps insufficient consideration within the Theravadin tradition and also within the lives of many people in the West.

## Long Retreats

On short retreats, a few days to a week, I have a standard way of working, emphasizing attention, insight and emptiness. On a long retreat, I discuss with the person whether there is any particular thing they would like to emphasize in their practice. They might seek to develop greater concentration or more heart qualities. Sometimes a person simply wants to work with choiceless awareness.

People doing long retreats are taking great responsibility for their own path and spiritual journey. Therefore I feel it is appropriate not to be an overpowering authority telling people what is right for them, what they need to develop. Some people see that their mind has a tendency towards repeated aversion or craving, and would like to dwell in more equanimity. Another person's inclination may be different. I let myself be guided by their directions rather than imposing my own ideas upon them.

Developing deeper states of concentration and levels of experience requires a longer period of time and a certain kind of environment and support. Often a long retreat will be the only place where people can find all these. However, I do not think long retreats are essential to insight, as insight has nothing to do with time. Someone could come on a short retreat, or no retreat, and have a deep level of insight. However, long retreats provide an environment where there can be a ripening and maturity of insight and qualities of consciousness in the heart.

## A Complementary Approach

I started practising meditation with Geshe Rabten, a respected teacher of Tibetan Buddhism, in Dharamsala, India. For several years I followed a very traditional Tibetan practice, including visualizations, reflections and whole sadhana practice. Later on I did several vipassana courses while I was still with Geshe

Rabten and more vipassana practice in longer retreats in solitude, as well as doing some group retreats. By then I was doing *jhana* practices and following various Theravadin meditation techniques.

After some years I totally left the formal practice of Tibetan Buddhism. However, its background, emphasis and more visionary approach I took with me into vipassana practice. It is still very much a foundation of what I both practise and teach.

A lot of Theravadin practice is about personal revelation and insight, especially insight into the characteristics of existence: impermanence, suffering and no-self. It is a path which brings certain experiences, openings and advancements. The danger is that we can become so entranced with the unfoldment of personal revelation that we forget the wider vision found in Mahayana Buddhism, which emphasizes the development of compassion.

Sometimes there does not seem to be much of a goal in the Theravadin tradition apart from the end of suffering and personal liberation. Later developments in Theravada such as loving-kindness meditation tend to be regarded as secondary experiences. Mahayana practice, with its emphasis on motivation and the intention of perfecting qualities of heart and mind, tends to support a broader foundation for the actual practice of meditation.

My two Buddhist backgrounds do not clash but actively complement each other. However, sometimes I find it difficult to teach giving equal emphasis to both. When I was training in the Mahayana tradition the teaching emphasized study, reflection, discussion and ethics. In the Theravada tradition as it is taught in the West (not necessarily in the East), the emphasis is more on emptying the mind and coming to stillness.

## Willingness

We need to reflect consciously on how to apply the dharma in our lives. In a retreat the main thing which supports change or insight is people's willingness to pay attention. If someone were to come on retreat with the idea of just having a vacation, then that is just what they would have. They might go to every sitting, but could just nod off. It is the willingness to pay attention that makes meditation alive and vital. This comes from the people on retreat; it is not inherent in the environment.

The willingness to pay attention is a primary factor in feeling we are on a spiritual journey. If we have the willingness to pay attention in all aspects of our lives, we will feel spiritually alive on a day-to-day basis. If we lose touch with the willingness to pay attention to what is happening in each moment, then meditation becomes a static activity which only happens when we sit on a cushion.

# further reading

Allione, Tsultrim, *Women of Wisdom*, Routledge & Kegan Paul, London, 1982.

Aoyama, Shundo, *Zen Seeds: Recollections of a Female Priest*, Kosei Publishing, Tokyo, 1990.

Banks, Findly, Ellison, ed., *Women's Buddhism, Buddhism's Women*, Wisdom, Boston, 2000.

Batchelor, Martine, *Buddhism and Ecology*, Cassell, London, 1992.

—, *Meditation for Life*, Frances Lincoln, London, 2001.

Batchelor, Stephen, *The Awakening of the West: The Encounter of Buddhism and Western Culture*, Aquarian, London, 1994.

Boucher, Sandy, *Turning the Wheel: American Women Creating the New Buddhism*, Harper & Row, San Francisco, 1988.

Buswell, Robert, *The Korean Approach to Zen: The Collected Works of Chinul (Master Bojo)*, University of Hawaii Press, Honolulu, 1983.

Chan Khong, *Learning True Love*, Parallax Press, Berkeley, 1994.

Chodron, Thubten, *Open Heart, Clear Mind*, Snow Lion, Ithaca, New York, 1990.

—, *Working with Anger*, Snow Lion, Ithaca, New York, 2001.

Cleary, Thomas, *The Flower Ornament Scripture (The Avatamsaka Sutra)*, Shambala, Boston, 1984.

Feldman, Christina, *Quest of the Warrior Woman*, Aquarian, London, 1994.

—, *Simplicity*, Thorsons, London, 2001.

—, *Woman Awake*, Arkana, London, 1990.

Friedman, Lenore, *Meetings with Remarkable Women: Buddhist Teachers in America*, Shambala, Boston, 1987.

Friedman, Lehore and Moon, Susan, eds., *Being Bodies*, Shambala, Boston, 1997.

Goldstein, Joseph, *The Experience of Insight*, Shambala, Boston, 1987.

Hurvitz, Leon, *Scripture of the Lotus Blossom of the Fine Dharma (The Lotus Sutra)*, Columbia University Press, New York, 1976.

Khema, Ayya, *Being Nobody, Going Nowhere*, Wisdom, Boston, 1987.

—, *When the Iron Eagle Flies: Buddhism for the West*, Arkana, London, 1991.

Kornfield, Jack, ed., *Teachings of the Buddha*, Shambala, Boston, 1993.

Kusan, Sunim, *The Way of Korean Zen*, Weatherhill, New York, 1985.

Mackenzie, Vicki, *Cave in the Snow*, Bloomsbury, London, 1998.

Macy, Joanna, *World as Lover, World as Self*, Parallax Press, Berkeley, 1991.

Murcott, Susan, *The First Buddhist Women*, Parallax Press, Berkeley, 1991.

Nanamoli, Bhikkhu, *The Life of the Buddha*, Buddhist Publication Society, Kandy, Sri Lanka, 1978.

Nhat Hanh, Thich, *Being Peace*, Parallax Press, Berkeley, 1987.

Palmo, Tenzin, *Reflections on Mountain Lake*, Snow Lion, Ithaca, New York, 2002.

Rabten, Geshe, and Dhargyey, Geshe, *Advice from a Spiritual Friend*, Wisdom, Boston, 1986.

Suzuki, Shunreyu, *Zen Mind, Beginner's Mind*, Weatherhill, New York, 1980.

Tae Heng Se Nim, *Teachings of the Heart*, Dai Shin Press, California, 1990.

Tsomo, Karma Lekshe, ed., *Sakyadhita: Daughters of the Buddha*, New York: Snow Lion, Ithaca, New York, 1988.

Yampolsky, Philip B., *The Platform Sutra of the Sixth Patriarch*, Columbia University Press, New York, 1967.

# glossary

*Anatta:* No-self, egolessness.

*Anicca:* Impermanence.

*Arhat:* A person who has attained Nirvana through freeing themselves from the origins of suffering, delusion and craving.

**Avalokitesvara (Chinese: Kuanyin, Tibetan: Chenrezig):** The Bodhisattva who personifies compassion.

*Avatamsaka Sutra:* 'The Flower Adornment Scripture'.

**Bardo:** The intermediate state between death and rebirth.

**Bodhi-mind:** 'Awakening mind', the aspiration to attain Buddhahood for the sake of all living beings.

**Bodhisattva:** 'Awakening being', a person who aspires to become a Buddha.

**Bojo:** Also known as Chinul, a thirteenth-century Korean Zen master.

**Buddha:** 'Awakened one', a person who has attained both Nirvana as well as the optimal capacity to help others.

**Buddha Amitabha:** The Buddha responsible for the creation of the western Pure Land through the force of his 48 vows to save sentient beings.

**Buddha Shakyamuni:** The historical Buddha Gautama.

**Buddha Vairocana:** The name of a Buddha; according to the *Avatamsaka Sutra*, the Buddha whose body is said to symbolically constitute the universe.

**Chan (Chinese), Zen (Japanese), Son (Korean):** 'Meditation', a contemplative form of Buddhism that originated in sixth-century China and spread to Korea and Japan.

**Chinul:** *see* Bojo.

**Citta:** 'Heart/mind'.

*Dana:* Giving, generosity.

**Dharma:** 'Law': 1) the teachings of the Buddha; 2) the truths referred to by the teachings of the Buddha; 3) the application of the teachings of the Buddha.

*Dhyana:* Meditation.

*Dukkha:* Suffering, pain, unsatisfactoriness.

*Dzogchenpa:* A person who practises *dzogchen*, 'great perfection', direct Vajrayana teachings aimed at activating primordial awareness.

**Eightfold Path:** Right view, right thought, right speech, right action, right livelihood, right effort, right mindfulness, right concentration.

**Emptiness:** The lack of independent or inherent existence.

**Five Hindrances:** Sensual desire, ill-will, sloth and torpor, restlessness and worry, sceptical doubt.

**Four Gracious Plants:** Orchid, bamboo, plum blossom, chrysanthemum.

**Four Noble Truths:** Suffering, the origins of suffering, the cessation of the origins of suffering, the way leading to cessation.

**Gelugpa:** A person belonging to the Geluk, 'Virtuous tradition', one of the four schools of Tibetan Buddhism, founded by Tsongkhapa in the fifteenth century.

**Guru:** *see* Lama.

**Guru Yoga:** The fourth preliminary practice in Tibetan Buddhism, having to do with the receiving of blessing from the teacher/guru.

*Hwadu:* A capping phrase, the central point of a koan.

*Jhana:* Meditative absorption, tranquillity meditation.

*Ju In Gong:* 'The owner of the body and mind'.

**Kagyupa:** A follower of the 'Oral Lineage', one of the four schools of Tibetan Buddhism, founded by Marpa in the eleventh century.

**Karma:** 'Action', causality; the law of cause and effect, sometimes interpreted personally as reward or punishment for deeds performed in this or a previous life.

*Karuna:* Compassion.

*Klesas:* Afflictions, any emotion or conception which disturbs and distorts consciousness.

**Koan:** 'Public case', a record of an encounter between a teacher and a student in which an experience of enlightenment is triggered. Used as an object of meditation in Zen.

**Ksitigarbha:** A Bodhisattva who made a vow to save people in the underworld.

*Kumnye:* Tibetan relaxation exercises.

*Lam Rim:* 'Stages on the path', a systematic presentation of the path to enlightenment as found in Tibetan Buddhism.

**Lama/Guru:** Teacher.

**Maechee:** Name given to Buddhist nuns in Thailand.

*Mahamudra:* 'Great seal', transparency, direct Vajrayana instructions for realizing the true mind.

**Mahayana:** 'Great vehicle', the spiritual path of those who practise Buddhism for the sake of all living beings.

**Manjusri:** The Bodhisattva who personifies wisdom.

**Mantra:** A mystical formula usually composed of Sanskrit syllables. It is often associated with a particular Buddha or Bodhisattva and is recited in a continuous and repetitive manner.

*Metta:* Loving-kindness.

**Nirvana:** The cessation of suffering, delusion and craving.

**Nyingmapa:** 'Ancients', one of the four schools of Tibetan Buddhism, founded by Padmasambhava in the eighth century.

**Pali:** The ancient mid-Indic language in which one of the earliest canons of the historical Buddha Shakyamuni is recorded.

*Paramita*/**Perfection:** 'That which has gone beyond.' There are six perfections that need to be cultivated in Mahayana Buddhism: giving, ethics, patience, effort, concentration and wisdom.

**Pure Land:** In Mahayana Buddhism, a realm created by the compassion of a Bodhisattva or a Buddha where beings may aspire to be born in order to complete the path to enlightenment under more propitious circumstances. The name of Chinese and Japanese schools of Buddhism based on such beliefs.

**Rinpoche:** 'Precious one', a title of respect given to Tibetan lamas of high rank.

**Sakyan Rules:** The eight special rules given to Buddhist nuns, the acceptance of which was the prerequisite for the establishment of the order of nuns.

**Samantabhadra:** 'The Always Good', the name of a Bodhisattva generally connected with action.

**Samatha:** 'Mental calm', a concentrated, equanimous state of mind in which excitement and dullness are overcome.

**Samsara:** The frustrating, repetitive cycle of birth and death.

**Sangha:** 'Community', the community of people committed to the practice of dharma, sometimes used exclusively to refer to ordained monks and nuns.

**Son:** *see* Chan.

**Soto:** 'Silent illumination', the Zen Buddhist line of transmission that traces its origins to the Chinese Ch'an masters Tsao-shan and Tung-shan.

**Sunim:** The Korean title of address for monks and nuns.

**Sutra:** A discourse given by a Buddha.

**Tantra:** A scripture describing Vajrayana practice.

**Tara:** 'The Saviouress', a female Bodhisattva.

**Theravada:** The tradition of the elders, the school of Buddhism widespread in South East Asia and Sri Lanka.

**Tientai:** Syncretic Chinese Buddhist tradition founded in the sixth century which regards the *Lotus Sutra* as the definitive teaching of the Buddha.

**Vajrayana:** 'Diamond vehicle', the path to enlightenment as described in the Buddhist tantras. A Mahayana Buddhist tradition widespread in Tibet.

*Vinaya:* The rules followed by Buddhist monks and nuns: ethical discipline.

**Vipassana:** 'Penetrative insight', understanding of the central truths of the dharma by means of meditation practice.

**Yamantaka:** A deity of the higher yoga tantras. The wrathful aspect of Manjushri.

**Zazen:** 'Sitting meditation'.

**Zen:** *see* Chan.

# Why Buddhism?

Westerners in Search of Wisdom

Vicki Mackenzie

**Why is Buddhism the fastest growing religion in the West?**

Vicki Mackenzie, bestselling author of *Cave in the Snow*, has been a Buddhist for 25 years. A skilled interviewer, journalist and author, she explores this question in the US, UK and Australia. Among those who speak candidly about the effects of bringing Buddhism into their personal and professional lives are counsellors and writers, a woman lama, a terminal cancer patient, a diamond merchant, composer Philip Glass, Professor Robert Thurman, and Buddhist luminaries Sharon Salzberg and Stephen Batchelor.

The stories present an intriguing reflection of Western responses to the Buddhist way – to its ideas of consciousness and compassion, work and worldly success, family and relationships, nature and death, reincarnation, and other faiths. At a time when Western culture seems overwhelmed by materialism and individualism, Buddhism is attracting thoughtful people seeking a wiser way to live, inspiring them with tolerant and practical ethics, joyful spirituality, and fellowship within the unity of life.

Vicki Mackenzie is a journalist with a broad professional experience in the US and Australia. She has studied Tibetan Buddhism for 25 years, and has published widely on the subject.

# The Spirit of Peace

A Fully Illustrated Guide to Love and Compassion in Everyday Life

His Holiness the Dalai Lama

*The Spirit of Peace* by the Dalai Lama brings together for the first time profound, inspiring thoughts by His Holiness on how to live a peaceful and happy life; world perspectives on faith, science, and religion; and the nature of life, death, and rebirth, among a wide variety of subjects. An intimate picture of his early life is revealed to us through unique autobiographical material, providing a personal portrait of the Dalai Lama in his own words. We also receive the benefit of his clear, accessible teachings, showing us how to cultivate wisdom and compassion in our daily lives. From discussion of his studies, the invasion of Tibet, and his meeting with Mao, to his views on travelling in China and his perspectives on Gandhi, we are offered a truly enlightening window into his world.

Illustrated throughout with full-colour photographs, *The Spirit of Peace* also takes the reader on a photographic journey into the rich cultural heritage of Tibetan Buddhism.

His Holiness the Dalai Lama is the exiled spiritual leader of the Tibetan people. He was awarded the Nobel peace prize in 1989. He is the author of many books on Buddhism including *Transforming the Mind*, *The Four Noble Truths*, *The Art of Happiness* and *A Simple Path*. He lives in Dharamsala, India.

# The Buddhist Path to Simplicity

Spiritual Practice for Everyday Life

Christina Feldman

Moments of peace and stillness give us a glimpse of how extraordinary our lives could be. Yet this sense of meaning and wonder is so easy to lose sight of in the hectic pace of modern living. In *The Buddhist Path to Simplicity*, Christina Feldman, an internationally renowned Buddhist teacher, shows you how to find harmony and balance by applying ancient Buddhist Wisdom to the here and now. The path of conscious simplicity she suggests allows us to fully recover ourselves, by rediscovering our sense of meaning and wonder.

As a mother, a layperson and an internationally renowned teacher, Feldman knows the stresses and strains of modern life. In this book she shows how to harmonize and achieve balance and how to apply Buddhist wisdom to the here and now. She addresses subjects of compassion, speech, effort, intention, mindfulness and awakening. The path to peace, she suggests, is not necessarily complex or arduous. If we simply turn our attention to this moment, it will speak to us of wonder, mystery, harmony and peace. She demonstrates that there is no better moment in which to awaken and discover everything our heart longs for than this very moment.

Christina Feldman is Co-founder and Guiding Teacher of Gaia House, and has been leading Insight Meditation retreats since 1976. She is also Guiding Teacher of the Insight Meditation Society, Barre, Massachusetts. Christina is a member of the International Board of the Buddhist Peace Fellowship and is the author of *Principles of Meditation*, *Way of Meditation* and co-author of *Soul Food*.

# Thorsons

## Directions for Life

www.thorsons.com